Innovative language pedagogy report

Edited by Tita Beaven
and Fernando Rosell-Aguilar

Published by Research-publishing.net, a not-for-profit association
Contact: info@research-publishing.net

© 2021 by Editors (collective work)
© 2021 by Authors (individual work)

Innovative language pedagogy report
Edited by Tita Beaven and Fernando Rosell-Aguilar

Publication date: 2021/03/22

Rights: the whole volume is published under the Attribution-NonCommercial-NoDerivatives International (CC BY-NC-ND) licence; **individual articles may have a different licence**. Under the CC BY-NC-ND licence, the volume is freely available online (https://doi.org/10.14705/rpnet.2021.50.9782490057863) for anybody to read, download, copy, and redistribute provided that the author(s), editorial team, and publisher are properly cited. Commercial use and derivative works are, however, not permitted.

Disclaimer: Research-publishing.net does not take any responsibility for the content of the pages written by the authors of this book. The authors have recognised that the work described was not published before, or that it was not under consideration for publication elsewhere. While the information in this book is believed to be true and accurate on the date of its going to press, neither the editorial team nor the publisher can accept any legal responsibility for any errors or omissions. The publisher makes no warranty, expressed or implied, with respect to the material contained herein. While Research-publishing.net is committed to publishing works of integrity, the words are the authors' alone.

Trademark notice: product or corporate names may be trademarks or registered trademarks, and are used only for identification and explanation without intent to infringe.

Copyrighted material: every effort has been made by the editorial team to trace copyright holders and to obtain their permission for the use of copyrighted material in this book. In the event of errors or omissions, please notify the publisher of any corrections that will need to be incorporated in future editions of this book.

Typeset by Research-publishing.net
Cover layout by © 2021 Raphaël Savina (raphael@savina.net)
Photo by Digital Buggu from Pexels (CC0)

ISBN13: 978-2-490057-86-3 (Ebook, PDF, colour)
ISBN13: 978-2-490057-87-0 (Ebook, EPUB, colour)
ISBN13: 978-2-490057-85-6 (Paperback - Print on demand, black and white)
Print on demand technology is a high-quality, innovative and ecological printing method; with which the book is never 'out of stock' or 'out of print'.

British Library Cataloguing-in-Publication Data.
A cataloguing record for this book is available from the British Library.

Legal deposit, France: Bibliothèque Nationale de France - Dépôt légal: mars 2021.

Table of contents

vii   Notes on contributors

xxi Foreword
Robert Godwin-Jones

1   Introduction
Tita Beaven and Fernando Rosell-Aguilar

5   Decolonising the languages curriculum: linguistic justice for linguistic ecologies
Alison Phipps

11   Dialogue facilitation: learning to listen
Francesca Helm

17   Virtual exchange: connecting language learners in online intercultural collaborative learning
Begoña F. Gutiérrez and Robert O'Dowd

23   The linguistic landscape: enhancing multiliteracies through decoding signs in public spaces
Margarita Vinagre

29   Translanguaging: navegando entre lenguas – pedagogical translanguaging for multilingual classrooms
Mara Fuertes Gutiérrez

35   Learning through wonder: imprinting wonder in language learning for lifelong engagement
Alessia Plutino

43   Learning without a teacher: self-directed language learning in the digital wilds
Ana Beaven

49   LMOOCs: free, self-access language learning on a global scale
Ana Gimeno-Sanz

Table of contents

- **57**   Open badges: recognising learning through digital micro-credentials
  Teresa MacKinnon

- **63**   Comparative judgement: assess student production without absolute judgements
  Josh Sumner

- **69**   Technology-facilitated oral homework: leveraging technology to get students speaking outside the classroom
  David Shanks

- **77**   Ipsative assessment: measuring personal improvement
  Antonio Martínez-Arboleda

- **83**   The translation turn: a communicative approach to translation in the language classroom
  Ángeles Carreres and María Noriega-Sánchez

- **91**   Action-oriented approaches: being at the heart of the action
  Aline Germain-Rutherford

- **97**   Digital corpora: language teaching and learning in the age of big data
  Matt Absalom

- **103**   Digital storytelling: multimodal meaning making
  Judith Buendgens-Kosten

- **109**   Gamification: motivating language learning with gameful elements
  Joan-Tomàs Pujolà

- **115**   Augmented reality learning: education in real-world contexts
  Mark Pegrum

- **122**   Automatic speech recognition: can you understand me?
  Susana Pérez Castillejo

- **128**   Speaking to machines: motivating speaking through oral interaction with intelligent assistants
  Joshua Underwood

134 Speaking with machines: interacting with bots for language teaching and learning
Müge Satar

140 TeachMeets: continuing professional development for teachers by teachers
Jane Basnett

146 Author index

Notes on contributors

Editors

Tita Beaven is Director of Innovation and e-Learning at Sounds-Write, an education company in the UK. Before that, she was a Senior Lecturer in Spanish at the UK Open University, where she worked for more than 20 years. She holds a doctorate in Educational Technology from the OU and is a Senior Fellow of the Higher Education Academy. Her research interests are in the areas of Open Educational Resources and Practices and online language learning. ORCID: https://orcid.org/0000-0002-9074-8789

Fernando Rosell-Aguilar is a Senior Teaching Fellow in Spanish at the School of Modern Languages and Cultures at the University of Warwick, United Kingdom. He holds a PhD in Computer-assisted Language Learning and an MA in Online and Distance Learning. His research focuses on online language learning, including the use of apps, Twitter, and podcasting as teaching and learning tools. Other research interests include the use of multimodal synchronous online conferencing and task design. Fernando is a Senior Fellow of the Higher Education Academy and has taught Spanish and CALL at UK Universities (The University of Buckingham, The University of Southampton, The Open University, and Coventry University) since 1996. ORCID: https://orcid.org/0000-0001-9057-0565

Invited author

Robert Godwin-Jones, PhD, is Professor of World Languages and International Studies at Virginia Commonwealth University and past Director of the English Language Program there, as well as Director of the Instructional Development Center. His research is principally in applied linguistics, in the areas of language learning and technology and intercultural communication. Robert has published widely in those fields, as well as regularly presenting at international conferences and offering workshops. Most recently, he has worked in the areas of mobile-assisted language learning, open educational resources, telecollaboration, and informal language learning. He writes a regular column for the journal *Language Learning & Technology* on emerging technologies. His most recent book, co-

Notes on contributors

edited with Richard Lin and I. J. Weng (2018) is *Internationalizing English Language Education in Globalized Taiwan*. ORCID: https://orcid.org/0000-0002-2377-3204

Authors

Matt Absalom is a university teacher and researcher, linguist, Italian language coach, translator, and published author. His current appointment is in the Italian Studies program at The University of Melbourne. He holds qualifications in music, education, languages, and linguistics, and his research and publication interests cover Italian linguistics, computer assisted language learning, languages education, and a variety of related issues in applied linguistics. Matt's university career in Australia spans three universities: the Australian National University, University of South Australia, and the University of Melbourne. In addition to his academic work, Matt has a background in teacher professional learning and in the development and leadership of overseas education programs to Italy. A passionate advocate for languages and languages education, Matt is a regular feature of languages-related events around Australia. He is a dedicated practitioner of hot yoga and has recently discovered the joys of running.

Jane Basnett has been teaching for 26 years and heads up a large Modern Languages Faculty at a girls' independent school near London. Despite the number of years at the chalk face, she has never stopped learning and undertook an MA in Digital Technology for Language Teaching which she completed in 2016. She has organised and presented at a number of TeachMeets over the years, both with and without themes, and orchestrated her first online TeachMeet during the pandemic.

Ana Beaven teaches English as a Foreign Language at the University of Bologna Language Centre. She has a PhD in Applied Linguistics from the University of Warwick, and her main areas of interest are intercultural language education, the use of technology in the language classroom, learner autonomy, and virtual exchange. She has taken part in numerous European projects, and was the coordinator of Intercultural Education Resources for Erasmus Students and their Teachers (IEREST). She is also a trained Dialogue Facilitator with Soliya and a trainer for Erasmus+ Virtual Exchange.

Judith Buendgens-Kosten is a postdoctoral researcher at Goethe University Frankfurt. They hold an MA in Online and Distance Education from the UK Open University, and a doctorate degree in English Linguistics from RWTH Aachen University, Germany. Their research interests encompass multilingual computer-assisted language learning and inclusive education in the EFL classroom.

Ángeles Carreres is Senior Language Teaching Officer in the Department of Spanish and Portuguese at the University of Cambridge. Her interests lie in the fields of translation and language learning. She has published a number of papers on these topics and, with María Noriega-Sánchez and Carme Calduch, is joint author of *Mundos en Palabras: learning advanced Spanish through translation* (Routledge, 2018), a handbook which explores innovative ways of using translation for language teaching and learning. Ángeles is also interested in the interplay between translation and philosophy, and she is the author of the monograph *Cruzando límites: la retórica de la traducción en Jacques Derrida* (*Crossing Borders: The Rhetoric of Translation in Jacques Derrida*, Peter Lang, 2005*)*, and joint editor of *Translation and multimodality: beyond words* (Routledge, 2020). She is also a literary translator from English into Spanish.

Mara Fuertes Gutiérrez, PhD, is Head of Spanish at the UK Open University. Mara has experience in teaching Spanish, Linguistics, and Research Methods applied to languages in Higher Education and she regularly teaches on teacher training programmes. Over her career, Mara has conducted extensive research in the areas of teaching and learning Spanish, historiography of linguistics, linguistic typology, and sociolinguistics. Currently, she is co-leading the Diasporic Identities and Politics of Language teaching strand of the AHRC-funded Language Acts and Worldmaking project, and is a member of the research groups Linguistics in Language Teaching and Grama4. She is the Membership

Notes on contributors

Secretary of the Association of Hispanists of Great Britain and Ireland and a member of the Executive Committee of the International Association of Spanish in Society.

Aline Germain-Rutherford is Vice-Provost, Academic Affairs, at the University of Ottawa and Professor in the Faculty of Education. She received a Doctorat de Didactologie/Didactique des Langues et des Cultures at La Sorbonne Nouvelle, Paris III, France, and is the author of numerous publications on faculty development, second language pedagogy, speech technology, and the integration of active pedagogy in e-learning practices. Dr. Germain-Rutherford has headed several national and international research projects, specifically on faculty development and multicultural issues in post-secondary education and online environments, and she has been a visiting professor and keynote speaker in Europe, North America, Asia, Africa, and the Middle East. She is a recipient of the 3M National Teaching Fellow Award, a Canadian Award that recognises excellence in teaching and leadership in higher education.

Ana Gimeno-Sanz is Full Professor of English Language in the Department of Applied Linguistics at the Universitat Politècnica de València, Spain, where she has also held various managerial positions. She has published numerous research papers on language learning and teaching, more specifically in the fields of English for Specific Purposes and Computer-Assisted Language Learning (CALL). Prof. Gimeno-Sanz is Head of the CAMILLE Research Group, devoted to research in CALL and e-Learning. In 2016, she co-authored the first MOOC for beginner learners of Spanish, delivered on the edX platform, and in 2018 she published the first upper-intermediate English language course, also on edX. Ana Gimeno-Sanz is Associate Editor of ReCALL (CUP) and member of the Editorial Board of Computer-Assisted Language Learning Journal (Taylor and Francis), as well as being editor-in-chief of The EUROCALL Review. She is currently President of WorldCALL, the world organization for CALL.

Begoña F. Gutiérrez is a foreign language teacher specialised in the teaching of Spanish, Italian, and English. She is currently writing a doctoral thesis at the University of León, Spain, which deals with the implementation of Virtual

Notes on contributors

Exchange in Foreign Language Education. She has taught in various educational institutions in Italy and Spain, and has recently participated as a researcher in the European Erasmus+ KA3 project EVOLVE which aims to promote the practice of Virtual Exchange.

Francesca Helm is assistant professor of English Language and Translation at the Department of Political Science, Law and International Studies. Her research is in the area of online communication and collaboration, language policy, ethical internationalisation of higher education, intercultural dialogue, and virtual exchange. She is chair of the Working Group on Education Innovation of the Coimbra Group of Universities, and is currently leading the monitoring and evaluation of the Erasmus+ Virtual Exchange pilot project.

Teresa MacKinnon is an award-winning language teacher and Certified Member of the Association for Learning Technology based at Warwick University, UK. She is experienced in technology enhanced learning design in secondary and higher education. She researches and designs to find solutions supporting student-centred pedagogy. She curates professional development resources for language tutors and is active on twitter as @warwicklanguage. An active advocate of computer-mediated communication and open educational practice, she is currently involved in the EVOLVE project supporting the mainstreaming of virtual exchange.

Antonio Martínez-Arboleda is Principal Teaching Fellow in Spanish and Co-director for the Centre of Research in Digital Education at the University of Leeds. Educated as a lawyer, Antonio started his university career in 1998 teaching Spanish Language. His portfolio of subjects grew over the years, as the focus of his scholarship evolved: from Autonomous Learning and Employability into Oral History, Critical Pedagogy, and Digital Education. He teaches undergraduate Spanish Language and Politics and on the MA in Digital Education of the University of Leeds. He has published articles and book contributions about, amongst others; the OpenLIVES Pedagogy, an OER initiative involving the production of podcasts that became a Final Year Option for Languages Students; Audio-visual Feedback; and Digital Poetry. Antonio is a poet, editor, and cultural activist. He is the UK delegate of Crátera and

Notes on contributors

directs La Crátera de Ártemis, the international festival on translation of poetry in Spanish, in collaboration with universities across the World.

María Noriega-Sánchez is a Senior Language Teaching Officer in Spanish at the Faculty of Modern and Medieval Languages and Linguistics, University of Cambridge, and a Fellow and Director of Studies in Sidney Sussex College. Her publications include articles and books on language pedagogy and literary studies, as well as Spanish language course books and digital material for the UK Open University. Her current research interests lie in the fields of language learning and teaching, and translation pedagogy. She has recently co-authored, with Ángeles Carreres and Carme Calduch, the book *Mundos en palabras: learning advanced Spanish through translation* (Routledge, 2018), and co-edited the volume *Translation and multimodality: beyond words* (Routledge, 2020). She was a co-convener of the CRASSH Faculty Research Group 'Cambridge Conversations in Translation' from 2015 to 2018. Further details and a list of publications can be found at: https://www.sid.cam.ac.uk/people/dr-maria-noriega-sanchez

Robert O'Dowd is Associate Professor for English as a Foreign Language and Applied Linguistics at the University of León, Spain. He has taught at universities in Ireland, Germany, and Spain and has over 40 publications on the application of Virtual Exchange in university and pre-university education settings. He recently coordinated the European Commission's Erasmus+ KA3 project Evaluating and Upscaling Telecollaborative Teacher Education (EVALUATE) (http://www.evaluateproject.eu/). This was a European Policy Experimentation which studied the impact of Virtual Exchange on over 1000 student teachers involved in Initial Teacher Education across Europe. Robert's publications are available here: http://unileon.academia.edu/RobertODowd and you can follow him on twitter @robodowd.

Mark Pegrum is an associate professor in the Graduate School of Education at The University of Western Australia in Perth, where he is the Deputy Head of School (International). In his courses, he specialises in digital technologies in education, with a particular focus on mobile learning. His current research focuses on mobile technologies, digital literacies, augmented reality, and mobile learning trails and games. His books include *Brave new classrooms: democratic education and the Internet*, co-edited with Joe Lockard (2007); *From blogs to bombs: the future of digital technologies in education* (2009); *Digital literacies*, co-authored with Gavin Dudeney and Nicky Hockly (2013); *Mobile learning: languages, literacies and cultures* (2014); and *Mobile lenses on learning: languages and literacies on the move* (2019). He currently teaches in Perth and Singapore, and has given presentations and run seminars on e-learning and m-learning in some 30 countries. Further details can be found at markpegrum.com.

Susana Pérez Castillejo, PhD, is Assistant Professor of Spanish Linguistics at the University of St. Thomas, in Saint Paul, MN. She is also co-founder of Extempore, The Speaking Practice App. She has been teaching language and applied linguistics for over 15 years in face-to-face, online, and blended environments. Her research focuses on experimental phonetics, second language speech processing, and the integration of computer and mobile technology for language development and assessment. Her publications have appeared in international journals, such as Language Testing and International Journal of Bilingualism.

Alison Phipps, UNESCO Chair in Refugee Integration through Languages and the Arts at the University of Glasgow, and Professor of Languages and Intercultural Studies. She is De Carle Distinguished Professorship at University of Otago, and was Distinguished Visiting Professor at the Waikato University, Aotearoa, New Zealand 2013-2016; Thinker in Residence at the EU Hawke Centre, University of South Australia in 2016; and Visiting Professor at Auckland University of Technology. She was Principal Investigator for the £2 million AHRC Large Grant 'Researching Multilingually at the Borders of Language, the body, law and the state'; Co-Director of the £20 million Global Challenge Research Fund project on South South Migration and Inequality; and PI on a recent Arts and Humanities award for £2 million for cultural work in the Global South. In 2011 she was voted 'Best College Teacher' by the student body, and received the University's 'Teaching Excellence Award' for a Career

Notes on contributors

Distinguished by Excellence. In 2012 she received an OBE for Services to Education and Intercultural and Interreligious Relations in the Queen's Birthday Honours. In 2019 she was awarded the Minerva Medal by the Royal Society of Philosophy. She is a Fellow of the Royal Society of Edinburgh, the Royal Society of Arts, and of the Academy of Social Sciences.

Alessia Plutino is a FHEA and has worked as Senior Teaching Fellow of Italian at the University of Southampton and as an Associate Lecturer at the UK Open University for many years. Her career has focused on the teaching of Italian at undergraduate level (both F2F and online) as well as Italian, French, and German at secondary level. She has multiple research interests, ranging from Computer Assisted Language Learning (CALL) and Telecollaboration, to the use of micro blogging (Twitter), MOOCs, CoPs, and PLEs. She is now an independent educator and consultant and continues to work within both undergraduate and secondary sectors as a language ambassador and technology-for-languages enthusiast.

Joan-Tomàs Pujolà holds a PhD in Applied Linguistics from the University of Edinburgh. He is currently a Senior Lecturer at the Department of Language Education in the Faculty of Education at the University of Barcelona (UB). He collaborates in teacher training courses at the Institute of Professional Development of the UB. His research interests focus on different topics related to Computer Assisted Language Learning (CALL), such as m-learning, telecollaboration, tandem learning, LMOOCs, e-portfolios for teacher education, and active methodologies such as gamification. He is the principal investigator of the realTIC Research Group. More information in his professional portfolio.

Müge Satar, PhD is a lecturer in Applied Linguistics and TESOL at Newcastle University. Her research interests are in the areas of language learning and teaching, especially in multimodal, computer-mediated communication via videoconferencing, TBLT, and social presence. In her research, she uses both quantitative and qualitative methods, such as social semiotics, interactional linguistics, and social network analysis. She has publications in Language Learning & Technology, the Modern Language Journal, ReCALL, and CALICO.

Notes on contributors

David Shanks is Lead MFL Consultant for the Harris Federation and works to develop the languages provision across 47 schools in London. He taught English in France and Maths/Computing in Norway before completing his PGCE at the Institute of Education, London, and has taught French for the past ten years. He has delivered Professional Development on a range of Initial Teacher Training courses, leads the Harris School Direct MFL Programme, and sits on the Association for Language Learning's national council. He has contributed to Oxford Education's MFL Blog and recently completed an MA at King's College London, including a dissertation that investigated the use of Oral Homework in MFL. Since December 2018 he has also worked as a Subject Specialist for the National Centre for Excellence for Language Pedagogy (NCELP). He tweets as part of the #MFLTwitterati as @HFLanguages.

Josh Sumner is an experienced teacher of Spanish and French now working as Head of Modern Foreign Languages at Dean Close School, Cheltenham. He is also an examiner and paper setter for major UK and international examination boards. He is currently studying for an MA in Education at the University of Bath, where his research interests include innovative assessment and increasing uptake of MFL post-16.

Joshua Underwood has been involved in Teaching English as a Foreign Language (TEFL) on and off over the last 30 years. He has also worked as an academic researcher at the University of Sussex and the IOE, London. His academic pursuits have focussed on the design of user experience and include decision support to help clinicians interpret automated analysis of brain tumour data; ways to better connect primary age children's home and school numeracy learning using some of the first tablets and IWBs; an app to assist with self-directed vocabulary learning; and participatory science learning experiences that bring together school children, teachers, outside experts, and technologies to support citizen science. In 2011, he co-wrote a review of AI in education that is acknowledged as the inspiration for Pearson's report: Intelligence Unleashed – An argument for AI in Education. In 2013, he co-edited the Routledge Handbook of *Design in educational technology*. In 2019, he gave an invited keynote for the IATEFL LTSIG pre-conference event entitled 'Speaking with AIs, feedback, and

Notes on contributors

being human'. Currently, Josh is a teacher and teacher trainer at British Council, Bilbao, and invited lecturer at Universidad de Deusto in digital competences for trainee secondary school language teachers. Josh enjoys spending some of his time playing with technology and ideas to support language learning.

Margarita Vinagre is Associate Professor at Autónoma University of Madrid where she teaches English Language, Linguistics, and Educational Technology. Her main research interests focus on the use of technologies for foreign language learning and the integration of virtual exchange for the development of transversal competences in Higher Education. She has published widely on these topics in specialised journals such as *Computers & Education, CALL, LL&T, System*, and the *British Journal of Educational Technology*. She is currently a member of the Editorial Boards of CALICO and the EuroCALL Review. She has co-ordinated research projects on virtual exchange with Trinity College Dublin, Dublin City University, The UK Open University, Hogeschool Utrecht, The University of Limerick, University of Hawaii, Manoa, New York University, and Columbia University. Currently, she is the main researcher in an international research project that explores the benefits of virtual exchange in CLIL/EMI classrooms.

Reviewers

Lina Adinolfi, PhD, is a Lecturer in the School of Languages and Applied Linguistics at the UK Open University. Her professional and research specialisms embrace both language learning and language in learning, with a focus on learner-driven language instruction (process syllabuses), lexical chunks (formulaic language), pedagogic translanguaging, and language-in-education policies and practices in multilingual contexts. She has extensive experience of teacher professional development using OER, MOOCs, mobile technologies, digital badging, and 360 video, with a particular interest in India and other South Asian contexts.

Zsuzsanna Bárkányi is a Lecturer in Spanish at The UK Open University. Zsuzsanna received her PhD in Spanish Linguistics from the Eötvös Loránd University in Budapest. Her fields of expertise are the interface of phonetics and phonology, and L2 pronunciation. She is a Fellow of the Higher Education Academy and a member of AGHBI and ELEUK.

Jane Basnett, see Authors' section.

Ana Beaven, see Authors' section.

Tita Beaven, see Editors' section.

Kate Borthwick is Principal Enterprise Fellow (Educational Innovation) in the Faculty of Arts and Humanities at the University of Southampton, UK. She leads the University's MOOC programme as Director of Open Online Courses for the University and chairs the University Digital Education Working Group.

Kirsten Campbell-Howes is the Chief Learning Officer for Busuu, a language learning community of over 100 million students worldwide. She has worked in digital language learning for nearly 20 years, for companies including Pearson, Macmillan, and English First. She has written several ELT textbooks for Harper Collins as well as editing series for many different ELT publishers. She has an MSc in Applied Linguistics from Oxford University, where she specialised in Global Englishes. Kirsten has taught English in China and Scotland and worked on language education in many countries, from the USA to Rwanda. She set up and ran the popular London Educational Games Meetup (LEGup) for many years, developing a special interest in games-based learning.

Anna Comas-Quinn, PhD, is a Senior Lecturer at the School of Languages and Applied Linguistics at The Open University, UK, where she has designed, coordinated, and taught courses in languages and translation for the last 20 years. Her research is in the area of technology-enhanced learning with a focus on open education in language teaching and learning, the use of open educational resources, and the development of open pedagogical practice amongst language teachers. She has co-edited two volumes on open practice in language teaching, Case Studies of Openness in the Language Classroom, and New Case Studies of Openness in and beyond the Language Classroom. She is also currently investigating the potential of online volunteer translation projects to extend open practice in the teaching of languages and translation, whilst fostering the development of digital skills and digital citizenship.

Barbara Conde Gafaro obtained a bachelor's degree in Modern Languages at the Pontificia Javeriana University in Bogota, Colombia. Her thesis was published in the Lingua Xaveriana Journal of the faculty of Communication and Language. Barbara also obtained an online diploma for a course on teaching Spanish as a foreign language at Universidad Externado de Colombia. After working as an English teacher for two years in Colombia, Barbara enrolled on the MA in English Language Teaching and Applied Linguistics at Coventry University, which she completed in 2016 with a dissertation on a blended MOOC integration. She is currently studying for her PhD on MOOCs for Foreign Language Learning at the UK Open University, supported by the award of a Leverhulme scholarship. She has published three articles based on her doctoral studies and has presented at national and international conferences.

Alix Creuzé is a teacher of French as a foreign language, trainer of teachers, and coordinator of the pedagogical and digital innovation sector at the *Institut Français* in Spain. She is co-designer of online courses at the French Institute of Madrid and other French Institutes and Alliances françaises around the world. She has also participated in different international projects related to learning French as a foreign language: *Funambule, Lire en français, Voyages en français, Visions de l'autre, Parlez-vous interculturel*, and *Mlang* (Mobile learning project).

Martina Emke is a project coordinator and an experienced English teacher, who taught in further education, higher education, and in a vocational school. For the European Centre for Modern Languages, Martina has worked as a teacher, educator, and (online) workshop developer in several projects which have supported language teachers in (further) developing their online teaching skills. After completing her doctorate in education, she is now an affiliated researcher at the UK Open University. Her research interests include language teacher education and professional development, networked learning, algorithmic education, the use of social media in language teaching, and learning and ethical social media research. Martina has published about her work and presented at conferences.

María Fernández-Toro, PhD, SFHEA, is a senior lecturer in Spanish at the School of Languages and Applied Linguistics at the UK Open University. María has been working in British Universities since 1989 and has taught French and Spanish at all levels. She has also contributed to the production of several online language courses and her teaching publications include the book DIY Techniques for Language Learners (Fernández-Toro & Jones, 2001). Her postgraduate teaching portfolio ranges from Newcastle University's MA in Media Technology for TESOL to the Open University's Professional Doctorate in Education (EdD), where she is currently supervising doctoral projects on assessment and feedback. She has extensively published in these areas and her latest research focuses more specifically on peer assessment and self-assessment. In both teaching and research, María is deeply committed to pedagogical innovation as a means of promoting self-regulated learning and empowering students to continue learning beyond formal education.

Mara Fuertes Gutiérrez, see Authors' section.

Marta González-Lloret is a Professor of Applied Linguistics at the University of Hawaii, Manoa. Her research focuses on technology-enhanced teaching and learning, especially the effects that technology has on the learning of L2 pragmatics and the implementation of technology in Task-Based Language Teaching. She has presented widely on these topics and her work has appeared in various handbooks, encyclopaedias, edited volumes, and journals of the field. She is currently President of CALICO, co-editor of the Task-Based Language Teaching, Issues, Research, and Practice book series (John Benjamins), and the editor of the Pragmatics & Language Learning book series (NFLRC).

Mar Gutiérrez Colón holds a Degree in English and German Philology (1995) and PhD in Second Language Acquisition (2002). She has been a lecturer at the Department of English and German Studies at the Rovira i Virgili University

Notes on contributors

(URV) in Tarragona, Spain, since 1996 and has coordinated the URV Masters programme in Foreign Language Teaching. She has led research projects in the field of applied linguistics and computer-assisted language learning and mobile-assisted language learning, and has published key articles in these fields. In 2013 she was awarded with the URV's Council's Award for the Teaching Quality and Innovation. She has supervised nine doctoral theses and has coordinated the European project StratApp (KA203, Strategic Partnership) on language learning and the use of mobile devices. For four years, she was the Vice-Rector for Internationalisation at the Universitat Rovira i Virgili, Tarragona.

Séverine Hubscher-Davidson, PhD, is Senior Lecturer and Head of Translation at the UK Open University. She has authored articles in journals such as Target, Meta, and Translation Studies, and is the author of the Routledge monograph Translation and Emotion – A Psychological Perspective. She currently serves on the editorial board of Perspectives: Studies in Translatology.

Teresa MacKinnon, see Authors' section.

Joshua Underwood, see Authors' section.

Foreword

Robert Godwin-Jones[1]

The rich variety of innovative approaches to language learning represented here points to one of the main characteristics of the learning environment today, namely the ever-expanding choice in strategies and resources that fit particular contexts. The contributions in this collection are, in that sense, tremendously helpful as they lay out what the innovation is and how it is used, but also are forthright about both the benefits and potential issues. While many of the innovations discussed here involve the use of technology, we should keep in mind that the newest and greatest technologies are not necessarily those most compatible with pedagogical needs and best practices.

One of the most exciting aspects of Second Language Acquisition (SLA) today is the opportunity afforded by extramural learning resources. These are opportunities for extending learning beyond the classroom or for self-directed autonomous learning (see **learning without a teacher**). This process offers informal, implicit language learning through interacting in activities such as social media, multiplayer games, online affinity groups, or extensive viewing of videos. Some learners may favor a structured approach, such as that offered through participation in an **LMOOC**, which provides a formal instructional environment online along with peer learner contacts. Interactions in the Second Language (L2) online with content, individuals, and communities can supply considerably more exposure to authentic L2 language than is available in the classroom or provided by coursebooks. The language learning potential of informal resources, such as social or streaming media, is enhanced by the emotional resonance often involved. **Learning through wonder**, which leverages children's natural curiosity about everyday objects into language learning, similarly can evoke emotional responses and enhance longer-term learning. Individual investment in learning is an aspect too of **action-oriented**

---

1. Virginia Commonwealth University, Richmond, Virginia, United States; rgjones@vcu.edu; https://orcid.org/0000-0002-2377-3204

How to cite: Godwin-Jones, R. (2021). Foreword. In T. Beaven & F. Rosell-Aguilar (Eds), *Innovative language pedagogy report* (pp. xxi-xxiv). Research-publishing.net. https://doi.org/10.14705/rpnet.2021.50.1226

approaches to language learning, involving learners in meaningful, real-life situations, often leading to highly personal multimedia projects.

An important aspect of L2 learning opportunities online is their multimodal character. That is particularly evident in digital media; where texting, social media posts, and other content containers allow for the seamless integration of texts, audio, and images. Using all available modes of communication to enhance narrative effectiveness is a hallmark of **digital storytelling**. Online gaming is typically multimodal as well, with often highly personal engagement often leading to interactions with other gamers beyond the gameplay itself (see **gamification**). Another multimodal activity that takes learners outside the classroom is the use of **linguistic landscape**, in which students are typically exposed to different genres and modes of presentation, most often in an urban environment. Another avenue for place-based learning is the use of **augmented reality learning**. This most often involves students in task-based learning, with goals such as solving a mystery or creating a cultural guidebook. This presents an engaging opportunity for combining the digital with the real world.

In engaging with the outside world, either through physical displacement or virtually, students are likely to encounter multiple languages, a phenomenon particularly evident in online environments. **Translanguaging** calls for new kinds of multilingual and multimodal literacies; it is helpful in developing multiliteracies for learners to gain metalinguistic awareness, understanding that language learning goes beyond a static set of grammar rules and vocabulary knowledge. One of the tools helpful in that process is for students to engage in **translation turn** activities. Translating is fundamentally a process of mediation, which exposes cultural fault lines, along with differing linguistic conventions and pragmatic behaviors. The use of **digital corpora** can also be helpful in gaining metalinguistic knowledge through having students induce patterns of usage through analysis of contextual examples.

While language learning using informal online resources can provide powerful learning opportunities for independent learners, an instructed learning environment can leverage those resources – along with the mentoring and organizing role of the teacher – to provide an optimal language learning environment. Language educators can model and guide the use of online resources in their classroom (or online). Teachers might take advantage of **automatic speech recognition** to have students experiment with **speaking to machines** or using chatbots to **speak with machines**. That can involve use of virtual assistants which can serve to practice pronunciation, test intelligibility, and engage in question and response.

Technology advances today supply other opportunities for enhancing oral and aural skills. One could take advantage of the ubiquity of mobile phones to have students record audio or short video clips to be shared with peers (see **technology-facilitated oral homework**). One of the methods that has proven highly effective in leading students to converse in the target language is **virtual exchange**. This involves students in communicating, either one-on-one or in small groups, with counterparts abroad. Virtual exchanges offer the valuable experience of engaging in real conversations in the L2. The interactions can build awareness of the importance of strategic and pragmatic competencies, the ability to use language appropriate to the context, as well as to be able to work around linguistic roadblocks. Multilateral virtual exchange often involves **dialog facilitation** through the use of conversation facilitators, who assist with both linguistic and cultural issues which may arise. That experience can bring learners into contact with cultural 'Others' and assist in the process of **decolonizing the languages curriculum**. In fact, an awareness of social justice issues has become increasingly recognized as an important element of instructed SLA.

One of the issues to consider with innovative approaches to language learning is how to assess student learning. There has been a growing awareness that it would be helpful to have both non-traditional methods of assessment as well as a variety of sources, whenever possible. That can translate in to continuous, iterative assessments (rather than big exams), the use of holistic assessment (see **comparative judgment**), or implementing **ipsative assessment**, judging student performance not on pre-determined criteria, but based on their incremental development. One of the recent innovations which can serve to document achievement as well as to motivate is the use of **open badges**. Other options include the use of portfolios, learning journals, or evidence from participation in discussion forums or other online activities. These and other assessment options and teaching practices, along with technology integration, offer many different approaches for teachers to consider. Professional development and collegial collaboration can provide (through **TeachMeets**, for example) support and knowledge through an exchange of experiences.

Which pedagogical innovation presented here may prove effective depends on the learning and teaching context. Implementations will need to be adapted to local conditions. It is in the nature of innovations that not all will be successful, but experimentation and risk-taking are as much a characteristic of good pedagogy as they are of effective language learning.

Introduction

Tita Beaven[1] and Fernando Rosell-Aguilar[2]

Colleagues at the Institute of Educational Technology at the Open University produce an annual report, *Innovating pedagogy*, now in its 9th edition, which looks at new and emerging approaches to teaching, learning, and assessment in a wide range of settings and subject areas. They highlight ten innovative pedagogies, and provide a research-informed summary of each one, as well as a list of further resources for those who want to find out more. Over the past few years, this has become an influential publication and we have long thought that it would be very useful to have a similar report that focused specifically on language teaching, learning, and assessment.

When Research-publishing.net announced their second *Give Back* campaign, we seized the opportunity and applied for the funding to produce this publication, which the editors kindly agreed to fund. We wanted the report to be crowd-sourced and, most importantly, we did not want to miss out any potential pedagogies that we might not be aware of. For this reason, we designed a survey asking language teaching practitioners to help us draw up a longlist of innovative pedagogies that they thought would have an impact on language teaching and learning. The survey was emailed to our networks of language teachers and researchers. In total, we received 42 responses from a range of practitioners. The majority of these (85%) were from the university sector, and the rest were from primary and secondary schools and further education. All respondents are involved in language teaching, mostly delivering teaching but also as teacher trainers and researchers, and have been teaching for at least six years (two thirds of respondents have been teaching for over 20 years). The respondents are located in a variety of international locations. A quarter of the respondents live in the UK and another quarter in Spain, which is unsurprising

---

1. Sounds-Write, Buckingham, United Kingdom; titabeaven@gmail.com; https://orcid.org/0000-0002-9074-8789

2. University of Warwick, Coventry, United Kingdom; fernando.rosell-aguilar@warwick.ac.uk; https://orcid.org/0000-0001-9057-0565

How to cite: Beaven, T., & Rosell-Aguilar, F. (2021). Introduction. In T. Beaven & F. Rosell-Aguilar (Eds), *Innovative language pedagogy report* (pp. 1-4). Research-publishing.net. https://doi.org/10.14705/rpnet.2021.50.1227

Introduction

given that our teacher networks are mostly located in those two countries. The remaining locations include France, Australia, Iran, Canada, the USA, Argentina, Mexico, Ireland, Hungary, Belgium, and Germany, although not every respondent indicated their location.

Participants in the survey were asked to propose up to three pedagogies that they thought should make it to the *Innovative language pedagogies* longlist. We emphasised that we were interested in pedagogies, approaches, and tools, and not necessarily exclusively in technologies, as some participants might have expected. We firmly believe that pedagogy, not technology, should be at the centre of what we do as teachers. A total of 106 responses were recorded, with considerable overlap as some respondents identified the same or very similar pedagogies. This list was condensed into 36 different topics, which were listed in a second survey to draw up the shortlist.

This second survey was again emailed to our networks of language teachers and researchers, and it was also shared on social media with hashtags relevant to language teachers to gain further exposure. Some 118 responses were collected. This time, the responses from the university sector represented 59% of respondents, which allowed more representation from other sectors. There was also a wider representation in terms of teaching experience, with 13.5% of respondents who have been teaching for 5 years or fewer, 17.8% between 6 and 10, 21.2% between 11 and 20, and 47.5% with over 20 years' experience. We were very keen to produce a publication that appealed to teachers in schools, further education colleges, and higher education institutions, as we are very mindful that we need to bridge the gap between research and practice.

The shortlist vote identified some clear favourites, such as virtual exchange, gamification, the use of voice assistants, and interaction with bots, all of which are present in this report. There were a small number of pedagogies and tools such as Content and Language Integrated Learning (CLIL) and flipped approaches that were also identified, but we felt these were already sufficiently well embedded into everyday practices to warrant a place in the final shortlist. Other pedagogies and tools elicited fewer votes, and as editors we selected those that we considered most interesting to our potential readership. In total, 21 topics were shortlisted which cover a broad range of pedagogies, approaches, and technologies. We also decided to include a last chapter on innovative continuing professional development practices around TeachMeets, and we hope that it will encourage those practitioners who have never attended one to do so, maybe to present their own favourite pedagogy or tool.

We contacted experts in each of the fields selected and asked them to submit contributions of up to 1,500 words. Each contribution includes the timescale, potential impact, description, examples, benefits, potential issues with the pedagogy, a look to the future, and a list of references and resources that readers might want to pursue further. We stressed the fact that this is not a research publication and that we wanted clear, jargon-free informative pieces.

The topics presented in each of the chapters cover a wide range of pedagogies, approaches, and technologies, and we have endeavoured to arrange them in some sort of coherent order. However, we expect readers to dip in and out of the chapters in whichever order they want.

As 2020 has demonstrated to all of us, it is impossible to predict the future! However, we have indicated for each chapter what the potential impact of the pedagogy, approach, or tool would be (high, medium, or low) as well as the timeframe for its widespread adoption or implementation. Some of them are ongoing, in the sense that we believe they are already being implemented quite widely, but we believe they will be even more so in the next few years. Others we believe will be widely available in the next couple of years (short term), within the next three to five years (medium term), or in the longer term.

We have produced this book in 2020 and are very aware that in the wake of the COVID-19 pandemic, many institutions have substantially increased their online activity and their experimentation with new tools and technologies, and this has had an effect on language teachers, many of whom had limited experience of online teaching prior to the pandemic. This has highlighted how varied the knowledge of online pedagogies is across language teachers, and provides evidence of the need for online teaching to be part of the teacher training curriculum.

This report explores new approaches to language teaching, learning, and assessment in schools, further and higher education institutions. It seeks to highlight and disseminate innovative pedagogical practices in the languages field in a clear, accessible way to inform and guide educators and policymakers to help regenerate and transform language learning. We hope everyone finds something inspiring and we would love to hear about which ones our readers try and how the experience goes.

Acknowledgements

We would like to thank all the authors who contributed to this report. They gave us their time and were willing to share their knowledge in their respective areas of expertise for this volume, sharing the spirit of the Give Back campaign. We would also like to thank the reviewers who provided feedback on the first drafts.

Most importantly, we would like to thank Karine Fenix and Sylvie Thouësny for the incredible work they do at Research-publishing.net and the generous nature of the Give Back campaign that funded this publication. Their enthusiasm, guidance, support, flexibility, understanding, and commitment to dissemination are second to none.

Decolonising the languages curriculum
linguistic justice for linguistic ecologies

Alison Phipps[1]

Potential impact	high
Timescale	long term
Keywords	decolonising, multilingualism, linguistic justice, indigenous, migration

What is it?

Decolonising the languages curriculum is a radical requirement to critically re-examine the way in which the languages curriculum has been formed in any context. It requires the examination of the power dynamics which have led to the dominance of certain languages over others and which languages are and are not accorded resources in schools, universities, and colleges by the state, by the military, by community programmes, and in families. Decolonising the languages curriculum requires what is known as a phenomenological double break.

First, it identifies the languages taught within the curriculum. Second, it considers, critically, why these languages have come to hold these positions. Third, it brings an ethical position to bear by bringing non-dominant languages into view and re-framing language experience and language education to both take into account and enable the learning of languages which have suffered significant attrition due to the colonial actions of the curriculum in the past.

---

1. University of Glasgow, Glasgow, United Kingdom; alison.phipps@glasgow.ac.uk; https://orcid.org/0000-0001-5958-1207

How to cite: Phipps, A. (2021). Decolonising the languages curriculum: linguistic justice for linguistic ecologies. In T. Beaven & F. Rosell-Aguilar (Eds), *Innovative language pedagogy report* (pp. 5-10). Research-publishing.net. https://doi.org/10.14705/rpnet.2021.50.1228

Chapter 1. Decolonising the languages curriculum

In so doing, decolonising the languages curriculum also, of necessity, deconstructs the normative assumptions which formed and maintained the languages curriculum of each age. For example, in the late 20th century and early 21st century the language curriculum in the UK was formed out of the Entente Cordiale and historical assumptions of the language of the nearest, dominant power which led to French being the language which took a central position in the languages curriculum, with German – the language of peace-making and of economic power in Europe – following closely behind.

Language curricula are a site of hegemonic struggle with different language groups – Chinese, Polish, Gaelic, Urdu, Latin, and Greek – competing for space for their language to be taught in what is already an overcrowded curriculum. In addition, as use-based arguments for subjects, and especially for languages, have dominated the postmodern curriculum, the languages granted curriculum space have largely been those which have made a case for their usefulness in economic terms. Dominant world languages, or languages with the greatest number of speakers, have made numerical arguments for their inclusion. Chinese and Confucian classrooms have been part of this development and it underlies the global dominant of English as a foreign language.

When the language curriculum is decolonised none of this is automatically given as a good way to proceed. Not only are the powerful and often violent histories of linguistic colonisation and dominance brought to the fore, but action is taken to re-orientate the curriculum towards those languages which have suffered marginalisation and attrition, and towards nurturing speakers – be they heritage, native, or simply communities of interest – in languages which have not enjoyed the same levels of resourcing as dominant languages.

Whilst in the past the resourcing of the curriculum for 'lesser spoken languages' or 'community languages' has been problematic, the technological availability of access to speakers, and the open-source nature of much of the voluntary work by those working to keep languages alive, has allowed communities of speakers to record and curate their language and heritage. Together with attention to cultural and linguistic rights, the problematic question of 'availability' of textbooks or access to speakers, is now merely a presenting issue, to the structural issue in decolonising the languages curriculum.

Example

An example of this is the development of Te Reo Māori in Aotearoa, New Zealand. Māori language activists have campaigned to have Te Reo acknowledged to develop immersion schools and to increase the societal and cultural space for Te Reo alongside English to such an extent that there has been substantive growth in learner numbers (Nock, 2006; Nock & Winifred, 2009). This has also been undertaken by teaching and learning methods which in and of themselves decolonise the language curriculum, such as not adopting the traditional communicative language teaching methods or other approaches – structural, functional, or grammar translation methods and instead using the methods indigenous to Māori – 'titiro', 'korero', 'whakarongo' – to listen, look, and speak – a pedagogy of embodiment not of cognition. In this way the methods instantiate on what Santos has termed 'The end of the cognitive empire' (Santos, 2018) and usher in sensuous methodologies in a sensuous curriculum. This represents a further phenomenological double break with the idea of a curriculum in and of itself.

First, it ceases to understand learning as linear and based on script and literacy. Second, it fosters approaches which privilege social and cultural habits, rather than individual prowess. Third, it does not see the 'curriculum' as a 'career or course' as in its Oxford English Dictionary definition, but as an ecological way of being in balance with other beings, human and more-than-human. A further example is the work of the Researching Multilingually at Borders project, whereby a common task of making a production dance piece with young people required all the languages spoken by participants to be in play (Phipps, Tawona, & Tordzro, 2016; Tordzro, 2017). The final production – *Broken world, broken word* – was made in at least 17 languages and allowed for the opacity and patience that listening, watching, speaking, and gradually becoming comfortable with learning to 'get the gist' made possible in terms of community formation, trust development, and equity.

Benefits

Decolonising the languages curriculum has the benefit of beginning in an ethical rather than a functional approach to language education. It does not value languages based on their economic potential, military usefulness, or political salience but rather from the perspective of any given community. It does not assume that the languages to be learned for such an ethical aim will be the same everywhere, but rather that these will be nuanced by history, society, migration, culture, and economics (Phipps & Fassetta, 2015). It allows for the experience of humility, which is necessary for all language learning, notably in those most used to wielding rhetorical power, and this fosters new habits of learning, development, and consciousness precisely in ways which can enable empathy and consensus building.

In an age of multiple crises, decolonising the languages curriculum, and reframing our notion of what a curriculum is, allows for an expansion of horizons and new world views for all, not least those which have been marginalised for centuries. It enables a stance that shows how we are situated within complex language ecologies and bound together in relationships formed in myriad languages, and that learning these is a key function of linguistic justice.

Potential issues

Any move to make curriculum change is subject to substantial resistance. To suggest, for instance, that Gaelic might be a medium for education in Scotland has led to considerable column inches of protest in the Scottish press.

The changes are steady, difficult, and for the long term. There is no quick fix to the programme of decolonising. Within the market models there is also no future, but what the work of decolonising is also showing is that it looks to a future beyond the relative newcomer, and already failing forms of global linguistic capital, by engaging philosophically with linguistic heritage, migration, and future questions of linguistic justice and human dignity of speech.

Looking to the future

> A decolonised languages curriculum is already present in what is often termed the hidden curriculum. It is present in the speech outside of education institutions and notably in artistic practice and rural contexts.
>
> The manifesto for decolonising multilingualism, which contains principles for action and approaches, focuses on praxis, on the need to experiment and try out approaches, not least to devise and improvise (Phipps, 2019). It offers a prospect of enhanced creativity and a breadth of learning contexts outside traditional institutions in future, together with technological and community resourcing of languages.

References

Nock, S. (2006). The teaching and learning of te reo Māori in a higher education context: intensive fast track immersion versus gradual progressive language exposure. *He Puna Korero: Journal of Maori and Pacific Development, 7*(1), 48-62.

Nock, S., & Winifred, C. (2009). Exploring synergies between Māori pedagogy and communicative language teaching. *He Puna Korero: Journal of Maori and Pacific Development, 10*(1),17-28.

Phipps, A. (2019). *Decolonising multilingualism: struggles to decreate*. Multilingual Matters. https://doi.org/10.21832/9781788924061

Phipps, A., & Fassetta, G. (2015). A critical analysis of language policy in Scotland. *European Journal of Language Policy, 7*(1), 5-28. https://doi.org/10.3828/ejlp.2015.2

Phipps, A., Tawona, S., & Tordzro, G. K. (2016). *Broken world, broken word: the show*. University of Glasgow, RM Borders.

Santos, B. d. S. (2018). *The end of the cognitive empire: the coming age of epistemologies of the South*. Duke University Press.

Tordzro, G. (2017). *Broken world, broken word: the documentary.* University of Glasgow, RM Borders.

Resources

A short manifesto for decolonising multilingualism by Alison Phipps: https://channelviewpublications.wordpress.com/2019/09/06/a-manifesto-for-decolonising-multilingualism/

Find out about researching multilingually at Borders, a project directed by Alison Phipps: https://gtr.ukri.org/projects?ref=AH%2FL006936%2F1

Dialogue facilitation
learning to listen

Francesca Helm[1]

Potential impact	medium
Timescale	short term
Keywords	intercultural dialogue, virtual exchange, facilitation, willingness to communicate, active listening

What is it?

When we think about dialogue in foreign language teaching then dyadic interactions, service encounters, or role plays that students might perform in a 'communicative' classroom come to mind. The kind of dialogue we are talking about here instead is a form of intergroup dialogue, that is dialogue as a method of communication that can be used to explore shared issues between groups from diverse backgrounds, dialogue that highlights the importance of people's lived experiences. For language learners, this kind of dialogue is an opportunity to communicate about themselves and their local identities, interests, and values and learn about others'. Online dialogue can bring people together to address questions that transcend their own borders, to explore common subjects but from the starting point of their locality (Canagarajah, 2004).

Intergroup dialogue is led by trained facilitators who are multi-partial leaders of a group process. Their role is to create a safe and effective learning environment and model tools for effective cross-cultural, intergroup dialogue. Facilitation tools include awareness-raising and addressing group dynamics, as well as using active listening skills such as summarising, mirroring, and reframing. Facilitators can bring critical thinking to a conversation by asking good questions, exploring

---

1. Università degli Studi di Padova, Padova, Italy; francesca.helm@unipd.it; https://orcid.org/0000-0003-2197-7884

How to cite: Helm, F. (2021). Dialogue facilitation: learning to listen. In T. Beaven & F. Rosell-Aguilar (Eds), *Innovative language pedagogy report* (pp. 11-15). Research-publishing.net. https://doi.org/10.14705/rpnet.2021.50.1229

terminology used, and addressing not only opinions but also actions and feelings.

Example

Language learners across Europe and Southern Mediterranean countries have been engaging in online facilitated dialogue projects through Erasmus+ Virtual Exchange. Every week for anything from 4-10 weeks (depending on the exchange) they meet with a group of 8-12 peers and engage in a two-hour dialogue session supported by trained facilitators. During these sessions, they talk about issues ranging from hate speech, gender and media, newcomers and nationalism, and technology and society – depending on the specific programme. Facilitated dialogues address topics on which participants may have diverse perspectives and experiences and which may be difficult for educators to address in the language classroom. Although participants may enter these exchanges as 'language learners', in the dialogue sessions they become language users and bring into play their multiple, intersectional identities as they position themselves in dialogues on a range of issues.

Benefits

Most language learners go into virtual exchange programmes with the aim of practising their foreign language, hoping to acquire skills and confidence in speaking. Many report initial anxiety as they enter a new space and are worried about actually having to use the foreign language; speaking to people they do not know. However, this anxiety is quickly overcome as they learn to listen to others, bring their experience or opinions to the table, and further understand the perspectives of others. The dialogue offers a genuine communicative context which can be meaningful and motivating for language learners and enhance their 'willingness to communicate'.

Through their participation in a facilitated dialogue exchange, language students acquire not only rich vocabulary related to the specific themes addressed, but also much more nuanced understanding of the issues than a textbook would offer as they are engaging with participants and perspectives from a wide range of socio-political contexts.

The most important thing participants report learning through facilitated dialogue is 'active listening' (Helm & van der Velden, 2020). This is not listening comprehension as a skill to master, a transaction where information is exchanged or transmitted and learners have to 'understand' what is being said. Rather, it is listening as a key to relationality, learning from and with others. This kind of active listening can bridge gaps between people but requires patience, attentiveness, and responsiveness (Schultz, 2003). Taking part in facilitated dialogue thus offers language learners opportunities for intercultural learning, engaging with difference, which can also lead to self-discovery.

Potential issues

To be successful, intergroup dialogue needs to be facilitated. Power imbalances, participants not feeling safe, or not feeling heard can affect the quality of dialogue, as can political correctness and orientation to consensus. Learning from dialogue is strongest when participants move out of their comfort zones and feel somewhat uncomfortable, but from a place where they feel safe.

Dialogue may not be suitable for those who have little familiarity with the language being used as the issues addressed are complex and nuanced. It is thus suited for those with intermediate or advanced levels of language rather than beginners.

A further issue is which languages are more commonly used. When bringing together groups of individuals from a wide range of countries in online facilitated dialogue, English is often the language that most participants will have in common as it has become the most commonly studied foreign language. In Erasmus+ Virtual Exchange, some exchanges have also been carried out in Arabic and some dialogue sessions in French, but much fewer than in English. For less commonly taught foreign languages it may be more difficult to find groups for facilitated dialogue from a wide range of sociocultural contexts who share knowledge of that language.

Looking to the future

> At the time of writing, Covid-19 has led to unprecedented levels of physical distancing, with more and more of our interactions and learning experiences taking place online. There is an increased demand for quality online learning experiences. The pandemic has also highlighted the interconnectedness of the world and the need for a greater understanding and social and political engagement with this world. There is thus an increased relevance of online dialogue which can involve language learners in meaningful social interactions.
>
> Looking to the future, facilitated dialogue could become a more common pedagogic approach in language education and be introduced in a wider range of contexts and with a greater variety of languages. A more explicit trans-languaging stance could be adopted in online facilitated dialogue to make it a more inclusive practice, as the multilateral and collaborative nature of dialogue lends itself to the use of multiple languages with participants supporting one another in meaning-making through translation, rephrasing, and a collaborative ethos.
>
> Language students, but also language teachers, can follow courses in online dialogue facilitation, thus developing facilitation skills which can be transferred both to the classroom and to many other online and offline contexts.

References

Canagarajah, S. (2004). Reconstructing local knowledge, reconfiguring language studies. In S. Canagarajah (Ed), *Reclaiming the local in language policy and practice* (pp. 3-25). Routledge. https://doi.org/10.4324/9781410611840

Helm, F., & van der Velden, B. (2020). *Erasmus+ Virtual Exchange: 2019 impact report*. Publications Office of the European Union https://op.europa.eu/en/publication-detail/-/publication/0ee233d5-cbc6-11ea-adf7-01aa75ed71a1/language-en

Schultz, K. (2003). *Listening: a framework for teaching across differences*. Teachers College Press.

Resources

Helm, F. (2018). *Emerging identities in virtual exchange*. Research-publishing.net. https://doi.org/10.14705/rpnet.2018.25.9782490057191

Helm, F. (2016). Facilitated dialogue in online intercultural exchange. In R. O'Dowd & T. Lewis (Eds), *Online intercultural exchange: policy, pedagogy, practice*. Routledge. https://doi.org/10.4324/9781315678931

Read about facilitated dialogue in this article: taking dialogue online by Rafael Tyszblat (pp.178-187). https://www.daghammarskjold.se/wp-content/uploads/2019/10/dd64-dialogue-web1.pdf

Watch and listen to students talking about their experience of dialogue: https://vimeo.com/80598254

What is dialogue? Watch this Erasmus+ Video: https://www.youtube.com/watch?v=ZsCbxPdEihM

Explore facilitated dialogue programmes: http://www.soliya.net and https://sharingperspectivesfoundation.com/

Learn about training for dialogue facilitators: https://www.soliya.net/programs/facilitation-training

Virtual exchange
connecting language learners in online intercultural collaborative learning

Begoña F. Gutiérrez[1] and Robert O'Dowd[2]

Potential impact	high
Timescale	ongoing
Keywords	virtual exchange, telecollaboration, e-tandem, blended mobility

What is it?

Virtual exchange is an umbrella term used to refer to the engagement of groups of learners in online language and intercultural interaction and collaboration with partners from other cultural contexts or geographical locations as an integrated part of course work, and under the guidance of educators and/or expert facilitators (O'Dowd, 2018).

Examples

The majority of reports in the literature on virtual exchange are based on bilingual-bicultural exchanges which involve two classes are studying each other's languacultures. Exchanges of this type generally reflect one of two models of virtual exchange: e-tandem or telecollaborative exchange.

In the e-tandem model, students are required to communicate in both languages during their interactions and to act as informal linguistic tutors to their partners,

---

1. Universidad de León, León, Spain; bferng@unileon.es; https://orcid.org/0000-0003-3059-237X

2. Universidad de León, León, Spain; robert.odowd@unileon.es; https://orcid.org/0000-0001-7348-135X

How to cite: Gutiérrez, B. F., & O'Dowd, R. (2021). Virtual exchange: connecting language learners in online intercultural collaborative learning. In T. Beaven & F. Rosell-Aguilar (Eds), *Innovative language pedagogy report* (pp. 17-22). Research-publishing.net. https://doi.org/10.14705/rpnet.2021.50.1230

providing feedback on their use of the target language. This model has been in practice for over 20 years (O'Rourke, 2007), and it is still common practice today, as evidenced by many reports of practice and the large body of research emerging from the related teletandem networks (Leone & Telles, 2016).

In the telecollaborative model of virtual exchange, exchanges combine foreign language development with an emphasis on intercultural learning. These exchanges typically involve tasks where partners present aspects of their cultures to each other, compare their cultural practices and perspectives, or engage in discussions based on shared texts. Telecollaborative virtual exchanges are usually integrated into students' classes, with teachers supporting learners in their online interactions.

Apart from these two models, there is also a growing interest in foreign language education in *lingua franca* approaches to virtual exchanges, which give learners the opportunity to engage in online collaboration with partner classes who are not necessarily native speakers of the target language. For example, this may involve students from Spain, Sweden, and Israel collaborating together in English as a *lingua franca* (O'Dowd, Sauro, & Spector-Cohen, 2020), or students from France, Germany, the Netherlands, and Spain using German as a lingua franca in their online interactions (Kohn & Hoffstaedter, 2017). These exchanges usually involve tasks which require collaboration on themes that go beyond explicit bicultural comparison. This approach to virtual exchange has gained popularity because teachers often struggle to find partner classes studying their languaculture, and also due to the questioning of the role of native speakers in foreign language education.

In university foreign language education, online platforms that provide 'ready-made' virtual exchange experiences for their students are also gaining in popularity. These platforms (e.g. *Conversifi* and *TalkAbroad*) function in different ways, but the majority connect foreign language students with native speakers in video-conferencing sessions, usually in exchange for a fee, which can be paid by the institution or the students themselves. They then provide the students and/or their teachers with recordings of the conversations, which can later be used as part of students' course evaluations. This 'outsourcing' of virtual exchange takes a considerable organisational and technical burden off the teachers, who no longer have to look for appropriate partners for their students. There is currently, however, a lack of reliable research as to how learners can develop their linguistic and intercultural competences through such un-mentored virtual conversations with native speakers.

Benefits

From the point of view of educational institutions, virtual exchange can be an ideal addition to institutions' internationalisation at home programmes, and can act as a useful complement to physical mobility programmes. Virtual exchange offers universities many benefits, including versatility, accessibility, and economic and environmental sustainability.

In the context of foreign language learning, there is no doubt that its greatest attraction is to offer learners an experience of authentic communication and collaboration with international partners. Virtual exchange offers learners the opportunity to develop their communication skills, overcome anxiety, adapt to different communicative situations, and develop the knowledge, attitudes, and skills of the intercultural speaker (Byram, 1997) – all in the context of their formal study programmes. Furthermore, the online modality of exchanges, combined with a formal educational context, offers participants the opportunity to learn media literacy and digital skills to appropriately consume and create content online, and to communicate and collaborate with international partners using diverse technological tools.

Potential issues

Establishing virtual exchange partnerships can be a demanding task, as it implies looking for suitable partners and then maintaining fluent and effective teacher-to-teacher communication and coordination throughout the entire process. Furthermore, big imbalances between the groups (levels of proficiency, areas of interest), the institutions (goals, expectations, needs, requirements)

Chapter 3. Virtual exchange

or the contexts (time zones, calendars) may negatively affect the success and effectiveness of the project. As far as technology is concerned, having back-up plans in terms of communication tools can be desirable to avoid communication breakdowns.

Looking to the future

Interest in virtual exchange has increased dramatically in recent years, and there are currently many organisations and initiatives which support the activity and provide training to educators who are interested in engaging their students in online intercultural exchange projects. The UNICollaboration organisation was established in 2016 to promote the research and practice of virtual exchange around the globe. In Europe, the European Commission has done much to promote virtual exchange through the Erasmus+ Virtual Exchange programme and the introduction of blended mobility in the new Erasmus+ programme, which combines stages of physical mobility with periods of online collaboration and exchange. In the US, organisations such as Steven's initiative and the COIL network also promote this approach to learning.

Starke-Meyerring and Wilson (2008, p. 222) warn that the success of globally networked initiatives such as virtual exchange depend on three key pillars – robust partnerships, innovative institutional policies, and new pedagogies for globally networked learning. This means that the future of virtual exchange will require the commitment and collaboration of three different groups of stakeholders in university education. First, international mobility officers will be needed to help establish international virtual exchange partnerships and networks. Second, university management will be needed to introduce innovative institutional policies that facilitate the integration of virtual exchange into university curricula and strategy. Finally, teachers will need to explore new pedagogies and classroom practices which incorporate virtual exchange projects. If these three groups can come together, then there is undoubtedly a bright future for virtual exchange in university education.

References

Byram, M. (1997). *Teaching and assessing intercultural communicative competence*. Multilingual Matters.

Kohn, K., & Hoffstaedter, P. (2017). Learner agency and non-native speaker identity in pedagogical lingua franca conversations: insights from intercultural telecollaboration in foreign language education. *Computer Assisted Language Learning, 30*(5), 351-367. https://doi.org/10.1080/09588221.2017.1304966

Leone, P., & Telles, J. A. (2016). The teletandem network. In R. O'Dowd & T. Lewis (Eds), *Online intercultural exchange: policy, pedagogy, practice* (pp. 241-247). Longman.

O'Dowd, R. (2018). From telecollaboration to virtual exchange: state-of-the-art and the role of UNICollaboration in moving forward. *Journal of Virtual Exchange, 1*, 1-23. https://doi.org/10.14705/rpnet.2018.jve.1

O'Dowd, R., Sauro, S., & Spector-Cohen, E. (2020). The role of pedagogical mentoring in virtual exchange. *TESOL Quarterly, 54*(1), 146-172. https://doi.org/10.1002/tesq.543

O'Rourke, B. (2007). Models of telecollaboration (1): eTandem. In R. O'Dowd (Ed.), *Online intercultural exchange* (pp. 41-61). Multilingual Matters. https://doi.org/10.21832/9781847690104-005

Starke-Meyerring, D., & Wilson, M. (2008). (Eds). *Designing globally networked learning environments: visionary partnerships, policies, and pedagogies*. Sense Publishers. https://doi.org/10.1163/9789087904753

Resources

Godwin-Jones, R. (2019). Telecollaboration as an approach to developing intercultural communication competence. *Language Learning & Technology, 23*(3), 8-28. http://scholarspace.manoa.hawaii.edu/handle/10125/44691

O'Dowd, R., & Lewis, T. (2016). *Online intercultural exchange: policy, pedagogy, practice*. https://doi.org/10.4324/9781315678931

Chapter 3. Virtual exchange

The EVALUATE Group (2019). *Evaluating the impact of virtual exchange on initial teacher education: a European policy experiment.* Research-publishing.net. https://doi.org/10.14705/rpnet.2019.29.9782490057337

COIL global network: https://coil.suny.edu/global-network/

Conversifi: https://www.conversifi.com/

Erasmus+ Virtual Exchange: https://europa.eu/youth/erasmusvirtual

TalkAbroad: https://talkabroad.com/

Teletandem:http://www.teletandembrasil.org/

Steven's initiative: https://www.stevensinitiative.org/

UNICollaboration: https://www.unicollaboration.org/

The linguistic landscape
enhancing multiliteracies through decoding signs in public spaces

Margarita Vinagre[1]

Potential impact	medium
Timescale	medium term
Keywords	signs, multimodality, multiliteracies, multilingualism, authentic input, cultural awareness

What is it?

The Linguistic Landscape (LL) is a relatively new field which draws from several disciplines such as applied linguistics, sociolinguistics, anthropology, sociology, psychology, and cultural geography. According to Landry and Bourhis (1997),

> "the language of public road signs, advertising billboards, street names, place names, commercial shop signs, and public signs on government buildings combines to form the linguistic landscape of a given territory, region, or urban agglomeration" (p. 25).

More recently, the type of signs that can be found in the public space has broadened to include the language on T-shirts, stamp machines, football banners, postcards, menus, products, tattoos, and graffiti. Despite this wider variety of signs, Landry and Bourhis's (1997) definition still captures the

---

1. Universidad Autónoma de Madrid, Madrid, Spain; margarita.vinagre@uam.es; https://orcid.org/0000-0002-4370-8880

How to cite: Vinagre, M. (2021). The linguistic landscape: enhancing multiliteracies through decoding signs in public spaces. In T. Beaven & F. Rosell-Aguilar (Eds), *Innovative language pedagogy report* (pp. 23-28). Research-publishing.net. https://doi.org/10.14705/rpnet.2021.50.1231

essence of the LL, which is multimodal (signs combine visual, written, and sometimes audible data) and can also incorporate the use of multiple languages (multilingual).

The LL signals what languages are prominent and valued in public and private spaces, and can reveal the social position of people who identify with particular languages (Dagenais et al., 2009, p. 254). Social actors (i.e. anyone who engages in intentional action) contribute to shape this space and construct their own identities in their interaction with it. The LL is also authentic input found in the social context which makes it an easily accessible and readily available resource for language and intercultural learning.

Incorporating critical explorations of the LL into the foreign language classroom can have important benefits for students' linguistic, pragmatic, intercultural, multimodal, multi-literate, critical, and reflective competences. For this reason, a particularly well-suited approach to underpin these explorations is a multiliteracies pedagogy (The New London Group, 1996), which requires, in line with Kozdras, Joseph, and Kozdras (2015), the consideration of visual, aural, gestural, spatial, and tactile modalities as equally important in a digital world that includes multiple modes of communication in a globalised world. Inclusion, diversity, and celebration of difference are central objectives in this practice that aims to prepare students for citizenship in the 21st century.

Example

The LL has been integrated in the Virtual Exchanges (VE) organised between fourth-year undergraduate students of English at Universidad Autónoma in Madrid, Spain, and second-year undergraduate students of Spanish at Columbia University in New York, USA, over the last three years (Vinagre & Llopis-García, in press). The exchange takes place in the first semester of the academic year and lasts for six weeks. During this time, students work in small groups (pairs and trios) carrying out tasks jointly.

The VE follows a progressive method approach (O'Dowd & Lewis, 2016), in which students from both universities first exchange information on WordPress about themselves (introductions) and four topics, one per week, relating to their cultures (stereotypes, history, and politics of their countries, slang and colloquial expressions, literature, cinema, and music).

In week five they meet their partners online in order to discuss, in a bilingual conversation, what they have learned from comparing aspects of both cultures in the previous four weeks. After the conversation has taken place, the students are asked to explore the LL of their respective cities in order to increase awareness of the prominence and value of the foreign language in the public spaces (English in Madrid and Spanish in New York). For this task, the students take and upload photos onto Padlet to create a visual representation of the presence of the foreign language in their urban environments. Then, they tag the photos by adding a short description and the location. After all photos have been uploaded, they are asked to categorise them by analysing official, public lettering (top-down) as well as commercial or private signs and posters (bottom-up) following Ben-Rafael, Shohamy, Hasan Amara, and Trumper-Hecht (2006). After this analysis, the students have to reflect and critically think of the *why, who,* and *for whom* of the signs: Why are these signs here? Who makes these signs and decides on their language choice? Who are these signs for? Who is the target audience?

In order to facilitate engagement with difference, the students' categorisation of signs, as well as the answers to the questions above, are discussed in the in-class sessions with the teacher and their classmates. Then, students are asked to write a joint bilingual essay with their partners in which they discuss the findings of their analyses and reflect on issues of power, majority versus minorities, discrimination, identity, community markers, and interest in benefits attached to language use in their cities. Finally, students create self-reflection videos in which they elaborate on what they have learned through this experience.

Students' comments in the self-reflection videos corroborate the potential of this activity to raise cultural awareness and facilitate the use of language in authentic

Chapter 4. The linguistic landscape

contexts. Students also describe the experience as a 'confidence booster', since they realise they can communicate effectively in the foreign language with a partner from another culture.

Benefits

By integrating the LL into the foreign language classroom, students are exposed to language use in authentic cultural and social contexts, which enhances their communicative competence and helps them develop positive attitudes and emotions towards the 'other'. The LL also provides students with a 'third space' in which diversity can be explored, identities can be negotiated, and social representation can be contested. This space is not a physical,

> "fixed space, but rather a fluid, dialogic space which is constantly constructed and reconstructed by participants who actively engage in dialogue and negotiate identities, not only through self-expression but also through mindful listening and the co-construction of meanings" (Helm, Guth, & Farrah, 2012, p. 107).

In this space there are multiple possibilities for interpretation, and differences "are not hidden or minimised but acknowledged and valued" (Helm et al., 2012, p. 107).

Potential issues

Despite the steady growth of studies in this field, the pedagogical applications of the LL in the foreign language classroom are vastly under-explored and therefore many are unaware of its possibilities. One potential issue relates to some students remaining superficial in their explorations and reflections. In order to minimise this, regular guidance from the teacher in the form of questions for reflection and in-class discussions can help them move from their comfort zones into deep explorations of 'otherness'.

Looking to the future

> The use of the LL as a pedagogical resource offers educators an excellent opportunity to create meaningful experiences for learners, since the use of public texts places literacy in a broader social context and connects learning to students' neighbourhoods and communities (Hewitt-Bradshaw, 2014, p. 158). In this context, the students can develop multiliteracies at the time they increase their awareness of, and appreciation for, diversity and difference. As this practice becomes more extended, practitioners will question the 'real value' of multilingualism and consider our duty to adopt a critical stance, one that involves connecting language with issues of inequality, oppression, and understanding.

References

Ben-Rafael, E., Shohamy, E., Hasan Amara, M., & Trumper-Hecht, N. (2006). Linguistic landscape as symbolic construction of the public space: the case of Israel. *International journal of multilingualism, 3*(1), 7-30. https://doi.org/10.1080/14790710608668383

Dagenais, D., Moore, D., Sabatier, C., Lamarre, P., & Armand, F. (2009). Linguistic landscape and language awareness. In E. Shohamy & D. Gorter (Eds), *Linguistic landscape: expanding the scenery* (pp. 253-269). Routledge.

Helm F., Guth S., & Farrah M. (2012). Promoting dialogue or hegemonic practice: power issues in telecollaboration. *Language Learning & Technology, 16*(2), 103-127. http://hdl.handle.net/10125/44289

Hewitt-Bradshaw, I. (2014). Linguistic landscape as a language learning and literacy resource in Caribbean Creole contexts. *Caribbean Curriculum, 22*, 157-173.

Kozdras, D., Joseph, C., & Kozdras, K. (2015). Cross-cultural affordances of digital storytelling: results from cases in the U.S.A. and Canada. In P. Smith & A. Kumi-Yeboah (Eds), *Handbook of research on cross-cultural approaches to language and literacy development* (pp. 184-208). IGI Global. https://doi.org/10.4018/978-1-4666-8668-7.ch008

Landry, R., & Bourhis, R. (1997). Linguistic landscape and ethnolinguistic vitality: an empirical study. *Journal of Language and Social Psychology, 19*(1), 23-49. https://doi.org/10.1177%2F0261927X970161002

O'Dowd, R., & Lewis, T. (2016). (Eds.). *Online intercultural exchange: policy, pedagogy, practice*. Routledge.

The New London Group. (1996). A pedagogy of multiliteracies: designing social futures. *Harvard Educational Review, 66*(1), 60-92. https://doi.org/10.17763/haer.66.1.17370n67v22j160u

Vinagre, M. & Llopis-García, R. (in press). Multilingual landscapes in telecollaboration: a Spanish-American exchange. In H. Maxim & D. Malinowski (Eds), *Spatializing language studies: pedagogical approaches to the linguistic landscape*.

Resource

EVOLVE project website: https://evolve-erasmus.eu/

Translanguaging
navegando entre lenguas – pedagogical translanguaging for multilingual classrooms

Mara Fuertes Gutiérrez[1]

Potential impact	medium
Timescale	long term
Keywords	translanguaging, linguistic repertoire, linguistic resources, identities

What is it?

Most of the world population speaks two or more languages, which means many classrooms are intrinsically multilingual. In addition, education in more than one language is currently being promoted across the world, and there is an increasing interest in exploring how bilingual speakers are educated, reflecting "the shift from monolingual ideologies in the study of multilingual education to multilingual ideologies and dynamic views of multilingualism" (Cenoz & Gorter, 2020, p. 300). This change in interpreting multilingualism is supported by the emergence of concepts such as translanguaging. Nowadays, the term *translanguaging* is used in various contexts (for example, bilingual and multilingual education, English-medium instruction, or language teaching, including Content and Language Integrated Learning, or CLIL; see Cenoz & Gorter, 2020, pp. 305-306). *Everyday* or *social translanguaging* refers to how multilinguals tactically use their whole linguistic repertoire for communication purposes. Rather than indicating what languages are,

---

[1]. The Open University, Milton Keynes, United Kingdom; mara.fuertes-gutierrez@open.ac.uk; https://orcid.org/0000-0002-9890-5945

How to cite: Fuertes Gutiérrez, M. (2021). Translanguaging: navegando entre lenguas – pedagogical translanguaging for multilingual classrooms. In T. Beaven & F. Rosell-Aguilar (Eds), *Innovative language pedagogy report* (pp. 29-33). Research-publishing.net. https://doi.org/10.14705/rpnet.2021.50.1232

translanguaging focuses on what multilingual speakers do with languages, which is to fluidly navigate across them. Therefore, the boundaries between languages become more diffused.

Pedagogical translanguaging or *translanguaging education* alludes to the "intentional instructional strategies that integrate two or more languages and aim at the development of the multilingual repertoire as well as metalinguistic and language awareness" (Cenoz & Gorter, 2020, p. 300), thus "a translanguaging classroom is any classroom in which students may deploy their full linguistic repertoires, and not just the particular language(s) that are officially used for instructional purposes in that space" (García, Ibarra Johnson, & Seltzer, 2017, p. 2). Consequently, the principles of pedagogical translanguaging can be applied to any classroom, at any level, and on any subject where more than one language is proactively being used (see examples in Cenoz & Gorter, 2015; García et al., 2017; Mazak & Carroll, 2016).

In the context of multilingual classrooms, facilitating pedagogical translanguaging represents a way to vindicate bilingual and heritage speakers' identities, and contributes to social justice. In the case of language teaching, pedagogical translanguaging plunges into the recurrent debate on the suitability of using additional languages, on top of the target language, for instructional purposes. It directly challenges the well-established conception of maximising the exposure to and the practice of the target language in the classroom by discouraging teachers and learners from using other languages they might speak or be familiar with.

Examples

One of the most detailed accounts on how a translanguaging pedagogy can be implemented in a variety of contexts is presented by García et al. (2017), who take three very different multilingual educational settings in the United States as examples of translanguaging classrooms (fourth-grade dual-language bilingual education, eleventh-grade English-medium social studies classroom, and seventh-grade English-medium maths and science classes). The idea is that learners' linguistic repertoires are resources, not deficits; the collaboration between teachers, learners, and, depending on the context, parents encompass (1) the construction of multilingual ecologies in translanguaging classroom spaces (hanging bilingual posters and signs, having books in many languages in the class library, using audio-visual materials in different languages); and (2) the planning and designing of class activities and assessment instruments that take into account a variety of strategies related to pedagogic translanguaging (among others, using translation tools to make meaning, allowing learners to express themselves employing their whole linguistic repertoires, facilitating reading and listening comprehension activities that require using two languages, etc.).

An example from a different context is given by Makalela (2016), who describes his work on implementing translanguaging practices in a university language course in Sepedi (an African language) for pre-service teachers who are speakers of languages from the Nguni group. The activities carried out include multilingual lexical contrasts, reading comprehension, and listening tasks using at least two languages (for example, reading in one language and answering questions or orally discussing the content of the text in another), or comparisons between different cultural conceptualisations across languages. Other strategies highlighted in other studies include the use of cognates, establishing comparisons between languages' structures and features, sharing linguistic biographies, or working with the local linguistic landscape as part of the learners' social context (Cenoz & Arocena, 2018).

An important point to make is that the language teacher does not need to master all the languages spoken by students to implement a translanguaging pedagogy, but

> " to enable the students to explore their ideas through the linguistic resources they possessed [and to rely] on their input to explain some of the language- or culture-specific construct [that might come up]" (Makalela, 2016, p. 18).

Benefits

When learning a new language, learners frequently turn to the additional languages they speak as a starting point or as a compensation strategy; implementing translanguaging practices leverages all this previous knowledge and highlights the differences between languages, supporting the development of learners' interlinguistic reflection and metalinguistic awareness, which, in turn, contributes to an increase in learners' linguistic competence and autonomy. Translanguaging has plenty of potential as a scaffolding learning practice, however, its greatest impact relies on its capacity to transform how multilinguals (and multilinguals in the making) perceive their relationships with the languages they speak and, ultimately, their identities and themselves.

Potential issues

The use of translanguaging pedagogies might be received with apprehension by both teachers and learners due to the introduction of additional languages into the classroom, thus, it is essential to manage their expectations appropriately and to encourage reflection on what would work for their multilingual learners. Moreover, pedagogical translanguaging requires careful planning to be conducted successfully, and that means investing in resources and in teacher training. Designing assessment instruments and rubrics in the context of a translanguaging classroom can represent a challenge as well.

Looking to the future

> Translanguaging pedagogies have already been successfully implemented in a variety of contexts. It would be worth it to continue highlighting its advantages and bringing educational authorities on board. The potential of translanguaging education and its long-term impact still need to be fully explored, thus, specialists need to keep on testing its validity via empirical studies, especially in contexts where learners might not share the same additional languages, and

> language teachers should be encouraged and given opportunities to consider how it can benefit their current practices and their learners.

References

Cenoz, J., & Arocena, E. (2018). Bilingüismo y multilingüismo. In J. Muñoz-Basols, E. Gironzetti & M. Lacorte (Eds), *The Routledge handbook of Spanish language teaching. Metodologías, contextos y recursos para la enseñanza del español L2* (pp. 417-431). Routledge. https://doi.org/10.4324/9781315646169-28

Cenoz, J., & Gorter, D. (2015). (Eds). *Multilingual education: between language learning and translanguaging.* Cambridge University Press.

Cenoz, J., & Gorter, D. (2020). Teaching English through pedagogical translanguaging. *World Englishes, 39*(2), 300-311. https://doi.org/10.1111/weng.12462

García, O., Ibarra Johnson, S., & Seltzer, K. (2017). *The translanguaging classroom: leveraging student bilingualism for learning.* Caslon. https://doi.org/10.21283/2376905x.9.165

Makalela, L. (2016). Translanguaging practices in a South African institution of higher learning: a case of Ubuntu multilingual return. In C. M. Mazak & K. S. Carroll (Eds), *Translanguaging in higher education. Beyond monolingual ideologies* (pp. 11-28). Multilingual Matters. https://doi.org/10.21832/9781783096657-004

Mazak, C. M., & Carroll, K. S. (2016). (Eds). *Translanguaging in higher education: beyond monolingual ideologies.* Multilingual Matters. https://doi.org/10.21832/9781783096657

Resources

Jim Cummins on Language teaching methods and translanguaging: https://www.youtube.com/watch?v=xrQQVkCINPQ

Ofelia García on Translanguaging: https://www.youtube.com/watch?v=5l1CcrRrck0

Translanguaging resources: https://www.cuny-nysieb.org/translanguaging-resources/

Li Wei on Translanguaging as a theory of language: https://www.youtube.com/watch?v=fnOx8GjPvj4&t=68s

Learning through wonder
imprinting wonder in language learning for lifelong engagement

Alessia Plutino[1]

Potential impact	low
Timescale	ongoing
Keywords	wonder, outreach events, inspiration, intercultural competence, cross-curriculum links

What is it?

Motivation to learn starts with wonder and the breath of wonder transcending curiosity, which Piaget (1969) defined as the urge to explain the unexpected and Engel (2011) as the urge to know more. When wondering, learners express the desire to know what they do not know, as well as what they already know. In the modern languages curriculum, a language learner who uses 'wonder' is driven by curiosity for the language(s); has questions about the place and the people; has a wish to know more about various cultures; and eventually become a lifelong linguist. When we introduce learning design based on the pedagogy of wonder, we implement an approach that allows learners to become agents of their own learning by initiating the questioning themselves. L'Ecuyer (2014) defines the emotional response to this type of pedagogy as a possible consequence of wonder, rather than wonder as such.

McFall (2013) has experimented with the effectiveness of the pedagogy of wonder by designing a five-step process: *anticipation, encounter, investigation,*

---

1. University of Southampton, Southampton, United Kingdom; plutinoalessia@gmail.com; https://orcid.org/0000-0001-5552-6763

How to cite: Plutino, A. (2021). Learning through wonder: imprinting wonder in language learning for lifelong engagement. In T. Beaven & F. Rosell-Aguilar (Eds), *Innovative language pedagogy report* (pp. 35-41). Research-publishing.net. https://doi.org/10.14705/rpnet.2021.50.1233

Chapter 6. Learning through wonder

discovery, and *propagation* to allow learners to go beyond the initial awe. Learning through wonder has been effectively used at primary school level in various subjects, but mainly in science, technology, engineering, and mathematics, and this article illustrates how activities using this pedagogy can offer an opportunity in modern foreign languages.

Example

A practical example of this activity is an outreach event that has been developed by colleagues at the University of Southampton (UoS). *El día de los muertos* (The day of the dead) is a holiday celebrated throughout Mexico which the outreach team at UoS has been using for over a decade as a teaching and learning catalyst event for learners of Spanish.

Local secondary schools and sixth form colleges are invited to share the experience with UoS language staff and students. A whole range of language activities are prepared to be completed on the day but also as take away tasks for further classroom development and practice: quizzes, puzzles, investigations, etc. Outreach activities like this one tend to be more attractive when facilitated by undergraduate language ambassadors, who can add to the excitement by talking about their own travelling experiences in Mexico during their year abroad or a holiday.

Benefits

This type of outreach activity works at its best when set up as a concerted effort between visiting schools and UoS, and using the five-step process described by McFall (2013). In Step 1, teachers are in charge of creating *anticipation* by using links with other subjects including religious studies, history, art, or philosophy.

Teacher and UoS staff both contribute to Step 2, *encounter*, by organising the visit day. McFall (2013) stresses the importance of focusing on 'how the quest begins' and, in this case, this is achieved with the introduction of the cultural and language elements of the Mexican altar (Figure 1) devoted to remembering dear lost ones.

Figure 1. Left: the altar display; middle: objects on the altar; right: Realia from Mexican tradition displayed on the altar. All pictures are kindly supplied by Irina Nelson, Teaching Fellow of Spanish, UoS.

With Step 3, *investigation*, the unknown and unusual objects, posters, pictures, etc. displayed on the altar, music, and videos, as well as presentations of the event and interactive discussion with facilitators, will contribute to make the encounter a multi-sensory experience, sparkling wonder and eagerness to know more. Then a concerted action involving all parties – the realia collected by UoS staff throughout the years and now displayed on the altar allows learners to have a fully immersive experience, as well as enhancing their language vocabulary skills, through the target language communication going on during the day.

Step 4, *discovery*, then follows and this is when learners are able to make connections between preparatory activities and what they see/experience/learn on the day, which enhances their willingness to investigate more.

Step 5, *propagation*, concludes the process by allowing learners to go back to their class and share their knowledge with others. As these outreach activities are for limited numbers, it is useful for attendees to be able to share their experiences and allow the same process to continue in a different context but using the same principles.

Potential issues

There are potential risks when using sensitive issues given that death is the topic of the outreach event described in this article, and therefore teachers should always run a pre-event risk assessment. It is hoped that the cross-disciplinary activities linked to this one will help make the event part of a cycle of interconnected activities whose scope will overcome some of the risks related to talking about death, and raise awareness of intercultural competence and understanding in a wider sense. Inspiring future generations to *wonder* about languages is getting more and more problematic according to the recent report published by the British Council, which sadly confirms that

> "Global English is perceived by teachers as being a growing threat to foreign language learning in England. Pupils have the perception that English is enough" (Collen, 2020, p.19).

This also negatively affects language learning uptake in secondary schools and sixth form colleges, where some parents seem to wrongly see Brexit and leaving the EU as an excuse not to encourage their children to study languages.

The domination of the traditional curriculum in modern languages and an excessive focus on testing at General Certificate of Secondary Education (GCSE) and A-level has also contributed to making languages an unappealing subject for some. These factors do not allow teachers any space for explorative approaches should they wish to divert from a traditional curriculum to include a pedagogy of wonder approach. Not even the use of technology, reported as a strong motivator in foreign languages (Woodrow, 2017), has managed to translate learners' initial motivation into genuine interest for languages. The 'Innovating pedagogy report' (Ferguson et al., 2019) expresses reservations about an education entirely based on technology and suggests that more creative and informal teaching methods –

such as learning through wonder – might allow experimentation and imagination in the way students can explore topics and experiment with languages.

Porter's (2020) research also provides evidence that starting from primary school, children enjoy opportunities to experiment with foreign language use, reinforcing the need for a concerted effort in providing an organic approach throughout the education cycle. This is where outreach activities come into place, linking primary all the way to higher education.

From primary schools, where "primary languages are embedded in policy, but not in practice" (Collen, 2020, p. 3), all the way to higher education, there is a need to counter the lack of inspiration and wonder in language learning. University language departments are already providing schools with opportunities to taste, learn, and experience a variety of languages through Language Days. In addition to this, as shown with *The day of the dead*, some specific cultural and meaningful events can offer inspirational opportunities for a pedagogy of wonder.

Looking to the future

> Language day outreach events organised for schools, if conceived as a concerted action and linked to primary/secondary/tertiary curriculum, could easily open the doors for new learning cross-curricular processes and ways to think about languages as a well-rounded subject, including cultural awareness and intercultural competence starting from a very early age.
>
> This article has provided an example of an activity which goes beyond the stereotypical picture of language learning and instead allows learners to think outside the box whilst making connections with other subjects and other ways of dealing with the same topic.
>
> By breaking down the risky topic of death and analysing it within different subjects, it allows a better understanding and sensitivity.

> It is hoped that by potentially reinforcing the importance of such activities, similar ones might be developed at all transition stages of education in order to create a supportive sustainable network between schools and universities to inspire each other and compensate for the flaws of a language curriculum which is way too rigid and assessment-driven.

Acknowledgements

I would like to thank my colleagues Irina Nelson and Jane Lavery from the Spanish and Latin American Studies department at the University of Southampton whose work in setting up and running talks on the in house annual event of *El día de los muertos* has inspired me to write this article.

References

Collen, I. (2020). *Language trends 2020*. British Council. https://www.britishcouncil.org/sites/default/files/language_trends_2020_0.pdf

Engel, S. (2011). Children's need to know: curiosity in schools. *Harvard Educational Review, 81*(4), 625-645. https://doi.org/10.17763/haer.81.4.h054131316473115

Ferguson, R. et al. (2019). *Innovating pedagogy 2019: Open University innovation report 7*. The Open University. https://iet.open.ac.uk/file/innovating-pedagogy-2019.pdf

L'Ecuyer C. (2014). The wonder approach to learning. *Frontiers in Human Neuroscience, 8*, 764. https://doi.org/10.3389/fnhum.2014.00764

McFall, M. (2013). *A cabinet of curiosities: the little book of awe & wonder.* Independent Thinking Press.

Piaget J. (1969). *The psychology of intelligence*. Littlefield, Adams.

Porter, A. (2020). An early start to foreign language literacy in English primary school classrooms. *The Language Learning Journal, 48*(5), 656-671. https://doi.org/10.1080/09571736.2019.1632918

Woodrow, L. (2017). Motivation in language learning. In R. Breeze & C. Sancho Guinda (Eds), *Essential competencies for English-medium university teaching* (pp. 235-248). Springer. https://doi.org/10.1007/978-3-319-40956-6_16

Resources

Arnot, C. (2011, May 31). A wonder room – every school should have one. *The Guardian.* https://www.theguardian.com/education/2011/may/31/wonder-room-nottingham-university-academy

'El día de los muertos' webpage at The University of Southampton: https://www.southampton.ac.uk/humanities/news/events/2011/10/31_day_of_the_dead_alter.page

Routes into Languages: www.routesintolanguages.ac.uk

Learning without a teacher
self-directed language learning in the digital wilds

Ana Beaven[1]

Potential impact	high
Timescale	ongoing
Keywords	self-directed learning, autonomy, polyglot, informal learning, community

What is it?

Self-Directed Learning (SDL) has been the focus of attention on the part of scholars for at least four decades. However, it is with the advent of technology and the possibilities offered by the Internet that researchers and practitioners have begun to look more closely at what students do autonomously to support their own learning outside of the classroom. Indeed, as Sauro and Zourou (2019) have recently pointed out,

> "developments in technology – such as mobile devices that afford connection and social interaction anytime and anywhere, social networking offline and online, horizontal patterns of connectivity that allow users to create natural bonds based on shared interests – all offer possibilities for user-driven, self- and group-initiated practices that redraw models of production, distribution, and reuse of knowledge" (p. 1).

However, much of the literature on autonomy in language learning focuses on developing autonomy within the language classroom (Dam et al., 1990; Little, Dam,

---

1. Università di Bologna, Bologna, Italy; ana.beaven@unibo.it; https://orcid.org/0000-0003-3289-3010

How to cite: Beaven, A. (2021). Learning without a teacher: self-directed language learning in the digital wilds. In T. Beaven & F. Rosell-Aguilar (Eds), *Innovative language pedagogy report* (pp. 43-47). Research-publishing.net. https://doi.org/10.14705/rpnet.2021.50.1234

Chapter 7. Learning without a teacher

& Legenhausen, 2017; Miller, 2009); and learner practices that take place outside the classroom itself are often seen – at least by language education researchers and practitioners alike – as supplementary to classroom-based teaching.

Indeed, an under-researched area is precisely what these "user-driven, self- and group- initiated practices" mentioned by Sauro and Zourou (2019, p. 1) are when they are totally independent from any connection to a language classroom or to a teacher. One such group of language learners, from which it is possible to observe these autonomous, user-driven practices, is the polyglot community – individuals interested in learning languages for their own sake, who willingly share their language learning strategies, resources, and experiences, acting as inspirational guides for other learners. For example, the *Facebook* page *Polyglots – the Community* has over 46,000 members, polyglot Olly Richards's page *I Will Teach You a Language* has over 53,000 followers, while Tim Donner's 2013 video *Teen speaks over 20 languages* has had more than 10 million views. As well as forming an active an online community, these independent learners also meet face-to-face during highly popular events such as the *Langfest* in Montréal (https://montreal.langfest.org/en/), the *Polyglot Gathering* (https://www.polyglotgathering.com/2021/) or the *Polyglot Conference* (https://www.facebook.com/PolyglotConference).

Example

An interesting example of a user-driven, group-initiated practice is *My Language Challenge*, where independent learners get together at regular intervals to study a language for three months. As the homepage of the website states,

> ❝❝[it] was created to be a community of language learners with a common goal - to improve our ability in our target language over a period of 3 months. It's called My Language Challenge because language learning is an individual thing. The way I learn a language works well for me but that does not mean it will work for you. We are all individuals so it differs from person to person. This

> challenge is all about finding out what works for you and doing it consistently with the help and support of a community of learners" (https://www.mylanguagechallenge.com/about/).

Thus, the participants choose the language they want to focus on, define their own goals, plan their study routine, and complete a daily tracker of their language learning activities to encourage accountability. If they start falling behind, their peers will often nudge them and encourage them to continue. Therefore, although learners may be studying very different languages, they can share strategies and provide support to their peers, through both the *My Language Challenge* platform, and the *Facebook* community page.

In addition, throughout the three months of the programme, regular micro-challenges involving all four skills ensure that motivation remains high. For example, once a month participants are expected to record and share a brief video of themselves speaking their target language. This is a way of both maintaining a sense of commitment and accountability, and tracking one's own progress.

Other micro-challenges include reading, writing, and listening tasks suggested (and voted on) by the community. This means they change from one challenge to the next, and may include writing a short paragraph every day for a week, listening to a podcast, or reading a short book or document (such as a simplified reader for less proficient participants, if these exist in their target language). Finally, once a month, well-known polyglots or linguists (but seldom language teachers) are invited for a live online discussion and Q&A session. Although learners may be studying very different languages, they share strategies and provide support to their peers through both the *My Language Challenge* platform and the *Facebook* community page.

Benefits

Self-directed language learning within a networked online community offers great advantages to learners. First, it enables them to study any language starting at almost any time without the requirement of a local course or at least a teacher.

Second, learners can work at their own pace and choose to work on skills that are more relevant to them and their needs. Third, networked communities offer learners a form of scaffolding in their endeavour – by providing opportunities to learn from others and with their support, find relevant resources and, through initiatives such as language challenges, set themselves time-bound goals and create a sense of accountability.

Potential issues

SDL is not for everyone. Inexperienced language learners may find it difficult, for example, to set themselves attainable goals, understand what strategies work best for them, establish workable routines, and manage time and expectations well.

Looking to the future

> An increased recognition of informal learning (see MacKinnon, this volume, on open badges) may encourage individuals to take advantage of the opportunities offered by technology and the Internet to independently develop their language skills, also in less commonly taught languages. At the same time, communities and networks such as those mentioned above, with their learner-driven initiatives, may become progressively popular, particularly among young learners.

References

Dam, L., Eriksson, R., Little, D., Miliander, J., & Trebbi, T. (1990). Towards a definition of autonomy. In *Third Nordic workshop on developing autonomous learning in the FL classroom* (pp. 102-103). University of Bergen. https://warwick.ac.uk/fac/soc/al/research/groups/llta/research/past_projects/dahla/archive/trebbi-1990.pdf

Little, D., Dam, L., & Legenhausen, L. (2017). *Language learner autonomy: theory, practice and research*. Multilingual Matters.

MacKinnon, T. (2021). Open badges: recognising learning through digital micro-credentials. In T. Beaven & F. Rosell-Aguilar (Eds), *Innovative language pedagogy report* (pp. 57-61). Research-publishing.net. https://doi.org/10.14705/rpnet.2021.50.1236

Miller, L. (2009). Reflective lesson planning: promoting learner autonomy in the classroom. *Maintaining control: autonomy and language learning* (pp.109-124). Hong Kong University Press.

Sauro, S., & Zourou, K. (2019). What are the digital wilds? *Language Learning & Technology, 23*(1), 1-7. https://doi.org/10125/44666

Resources

Bouchard, P. (2009). Pedagogy without a teacher: what are the limits. *International Journal of Self-Directed Learning, 6*(2), 13-22.

Italki: https://www.italki.com

My Language Challenge: https://www.mylanguagechallenge.com

'Polyglots – The Community' Facebook page: https://www.facebook.com/groups/polygotcommunity/

LMOOCs
free, self-access language learning on a global scale

Ana Gimeno-Sanz[1]

Potential impact	high
Timescale	ongoing
Keywords	LMOOCs, global audience, autonomous learning, self-regulation, self-access

What is it?

Massive Open Online Language Courses, also commonly known as Language MOOCs or LMOOCs, are online courses offered for a limited period of time by higher education institutions worldwide for anybody wishing to learn a foreign language. The average duration of these courses is between four and six weeks, and approximately three to five weekly study hours are required. Because of their duration, LMOOCs often focus on specific aspects of the target language, e.g. academic writing, improving pronunciation, written communication for the workplace, preparation for specific language examinations, survival language skills, etc. There are also abundant introductory courses focusing on basic language performance. Enrolment is free but these courses are usually not eligible for credit; however, learners may purchase a certification, which is normally moderately priced. Enrolment is not restricted by age, qualifications, or geographic location, conditions that nurture their 'massiveness'. MOOCs are delivered through online platforms which are based on the template approach to software authoring, that is, multimedia content is inserted into templates by materials writers. MOOCs that follow a course format are known as xMOOCs (x stands for eXtended). They include a syllabus and are organised according

---

1. Universitat Politècnica de València, Valencia, Spain; agimeno@upvnet.upv.es; https://orcid.org/0000-0003-3366-0729

How to cite: Gimeno-Sanz, A. (2021). LMOOCs: free, self-access language learning on a global scale. In T. Beaven & F. Rosell-Aguilar (Eds), *Innovative language pedagogy report* (pp. 49-55). Research-publishing.net. https://doi.org/10.14705/rpnet.2021.50.1235

Chapter 8. LMOOCs

to a set schedule; moreover, learners usually have access to some instructor guidance. On occasions, after the first edition of the scheduled course, some LMOOCs are made available on a self-access basis. This means that learners are free to set their own pace and organise their study at will. The onus of learning is therefore on the student. Most MOOCs are based on micro-lessons delivered through short audio or video clips followed by exercises, activities, and reading material. Most LMOOCs also include assignments, tests, or quizzes that are either automatically assessed or peer-assessed by means of rubrics. Grading is also provided, and students can oversee their performance through an automatic scoring system.

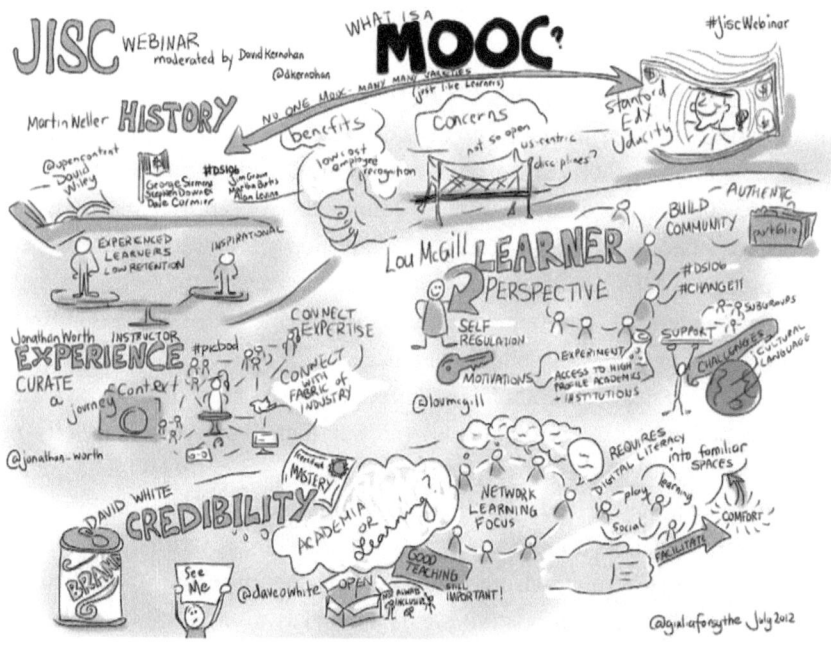

Figure 1. Illustration of the many attributes of MOOCs (CC0, Giulia Forsythe, https://www.flickr.com/photos/gforsythe/7549370822)

Among their many benefits, MOOCs allow learners to easily return to course materials as needed if access remains open. Through the course Forum, learners can connect with global learners and engage in communication through their common target language. They also have the opportunity of giving and receiving feedback from peers. Most LMOOCs are based on effective instructional design criteria. See Figure 1 above for a sketchnote of a webinar on MOOCs and the pedagogical issues around their use.

Example

To date, there are several examples of effectively designed MOOCs that facilitate the development of communicative language competences. The *Professional Certificate in Basic Spanish* (Figure 2), which comprises three MOOCs: *Getting Started*, *One step further*, and *Getting there* (see the resources section below for links), is an example designed by language specialists from Universitat Politècnica de València (UPV), Spain, delivered via the edX.org platform.

These Basic Spanish MOOCs provide

> a general understanding of common words and phrases, as well as basic grammar, Spanish pronunciation, and conversation skills, allowing [learners] to communicate in everyday situations according to the A2 proficiency level (elementary) as described in the Common European Framework of Reference for Languages" (Programme overview, https://stage.edx.org/professional-certificate/upvalenciax-basic-spanish).

Although these courses are now available on a self-paced basis, learners can contact a teaching assistant via the Forum to ask questions. To date, these MOOCs have attracted just under 350,000 learners from a range of 206 countries, and approximately 10% have completed and successfully passed the graded tests.

Through a post course questionnaire, 77% of the respondents indicated that the reason for not completing the course was due to time constraints. In terms of learner satisfaction, *Basic Spanish: Getting Started* is listed on Class Central's Best Online Courses of All Time ranking (2020) and on the 100 Most Popular Online Courses of All Time ranking (2020). Additionally, it was also listed among the 100 Most Popular Courses During the 2020 COVID-19 Pandemic. All figures relate to Class Central's database of over 15,000 MOOCs.

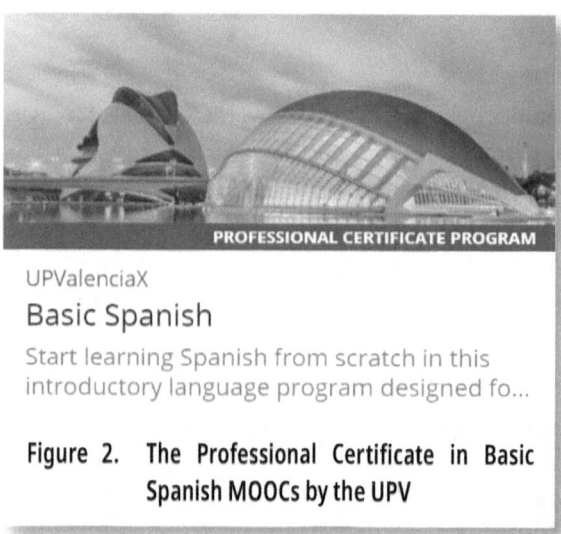

Figure 2. The Professional Certificate in Basic Spanish MOOCs by the UPV

Benefits

The prime benefits of MOOCs are precisely their openness and massiveness, that is, the possibility of reaching out to a vast and diverse audience worldwide, and in particular to disadvantaged groups in remote areas of the world where formal education may be limited. Globally dispersed cohorts can communicate through the delivery platform, thus creating a sense of conceptual *belonging*, as well as being part of a community of practice where common experience can be shared.

Despite the fact that MOOCs are designed for autonomous learning, they can also be integrated as self-access materials in a taught course to reinforce language practice or as the work to be conducted outside the classroom in a flipped teaching scenario. For instance, after having learners watch the video micro-lessons – which are often self-contained learning objects – and complete the exercises outside class hours, class time can be devoted to solving problems, extension tasks, and, on the whole, participatory activities.

MOOC platforms are self-contained systems and do not require additional plug-ins or add-ons for full functionality. Additionally, technical requirements are minimal so they can be used in areas of the world with limited technological access and development.

Potential issues

MOOCs are particularly suited to self-access or informal learning, which in most cases means that learners have to self-regulate their learning, very much relying on cognitive and resource management strategies, the latter to manage time, study environment, and the resources provided.

Because MOOC platforms are neither discipline-oriented nor dedicated online language learning environments, there are many limitations in terms of practising productive skills, i.e. speaking and writing. One of the drawbacks is that authentic language practice is limited but, if integrated into a regular course, extra speaking practice can be incorporated as an in-class activity. Alternatively, learners can sign up for private online tutoring offered through a variety of platforms or use online language exchange sites.

Looking to the future

> Progressively, more LMOOCs will be on offer despite the challenges involved. MOOCs have demonstrated that they offer valuable educational opportunities to millions of potential students, and many universities have started awarding accreditation at various levels (OEDb, n.d.). This means that learners around the world can register for formal education and benefit from high-quality technology-enhanced distance learning. Moreover, LMOOCs in

> particular are a means of widening participation in mobility and study opportunities, and can lead to enhanced employability. This belief was conveyed in the questionnaires given to UPV LMOOC learners: 15% of the respondents in the pre-questionnaire of the beginners' Spanish MOOC said their motivation to enrol was to improve their job prospects.
>
> As well as providing learning for the most popular languages in the world, these platforms provide an unquestionable potential, both in terms of promotion and sustainability, for specialists to develop and learners to delve into courses for less commonly-taught languages.
>
> Lastly, as MOOC platforms improve, better social tools are being embedded (for example peer grading is increasingly automated) and progress in building functionality to allow personalisation is being made (Quora, 2017).

References

OEDb. (n.d.). *The future of MOOCs*. https://oedb.org/ilibrarian/the-future-of-moocs/?

Quora. (2017, March 23). The future of massively open online courses (MOOCs). *Forbes*. https://www.forbes.com/sites/quora/2017/03/23/the-future-of-massively-open-online-courses-moocs/?sh=44c6e4686b83

Resources

Class Central: https://www.classcentral.com/ is a search engine and reviews site for free MOOCs.

Dixon, E., & Thomas, M. (2015). (Eds). *Researching language learner interactions online: from social media to MOOCs*. Computer Assisted Language Instruction Consortium.

Gimeno-Sanz, A. (2017). Designing a MOOC for learners of Spanish: exploring learner usage and satisfaction. In K. Borthwick, L. Bradley & S. Thouësny (Eds), *CALL in a climate of change: adapting to turbulent global conditions – short papers from EUROCALL 2017* (pp. 122-127). Research-publishing.net. https://doi.org/10.14705/rpnet.2017.eurocall2017.700

Gimeno-Sanz, A. (2020). Analysing learner motivation. *Conference Proceedings of the 10th International Conference on The Future of Education* (pp. 303-308). Filodiritto Editore. https://conference.pixel-online.net/FOE/conferenceproceedings.php

Gimeno-Sanz, A., Navarro-Laboulais, C., & Despujol-Zabala, I. (2017). Additional functionalities to convert an xMOOC into an xLMOOC. In C. Delgado Kloos, P Jermann, M. Pérez-Sanagustín, D. T. Seaton & S. White (Eds), *EMOOCs 2017 Conference Proceedings,* LNCS 10254 (pp. 48-57). Springer International Publishing AG. https://doi.org/10.1007/978-3-319-59044-8_6

Martín-Monje, E., & Bárcena, E. (2014). (Eds). *Language MOOCs: providing learning, transcending boundaries.* De Gruyter Open.

Professional Certificate in basic Spanish MOOCs by the Universitat Politècnica de València: https://www.edx.org/professional-certificate/upvalenciax-basic-spanish

Professional Certificate in upper-intermediate English by the Universitat Politècnica de València: https://www.edx.org/professional-certificate/upvalenciax-upper-intermediate-english

List of major MOOC providers hosting language courses:
Coursera: https://www.coursera.org/
edX: https://www.edx.org/
FutureLearn: https://www.futurelearn.com/
Miriadax: https://miriadax.net/home

Open badges
recognising learning through digital micro-credentials

Teresa MacKinnon[1]

Potential impact	medium
Timescale	medium term
Keywords	open badges, certification, validation, meta-data, micro-credentials

What is it?

Open badges are a 21st-century solution to the shortcomings of paper certificates in the age of digital, online identity management. These small visual signifiers which carry hard-coded meta-data can be issued by anyone in order to recognise achievement or participation in formal or informal activities. They link back directly to the issuer, the criteria for award, and the evidence. The learner can collect and display their open badges online to reveal their journey and discover new opportunities. Open badges emerged from the Badges for Lifelong Learning Competition in 2011 funded by the MacArthur Foundation and administered by HASTAC in collaboration with the Mozilla Foundation (MacArthur Foundation, 2012). The aim was to provide a "powerful new tool for identifying and validating the rich array of people's skills, knowledge, accomplishments, and competencies […to] inspire new pathways to learning and connect learners to opportunities, resources, and one another" (HASTAC, 2020, n.p.). The open badge infrastructure is based on an open source set of standards which have enabled the 'baking' of meta-data within a digital image through the use of an open badge platform. Open badge platforms are free to access, at least initially,

---

1. University of Warwick, Coventry, United Kingdom; profteresamac@gmail.com; https://orcid.org/0000-0002-1701-3727

How to cite: MacKinnon, T. (2021). Open badges: recognising learning through digital micro-credentials. In T. Beaven & F. Rosell-Aguilar (Eds), *Innovative language pedagogy report* (pp. 57-61). Research-publishing.net. https://doi.org/10.14705/rpnet.2021.50.1236

Chapter 9. Open badges

offering educators the opportunity to create visual, shareable micro-credentials which recognise a learner's journey.

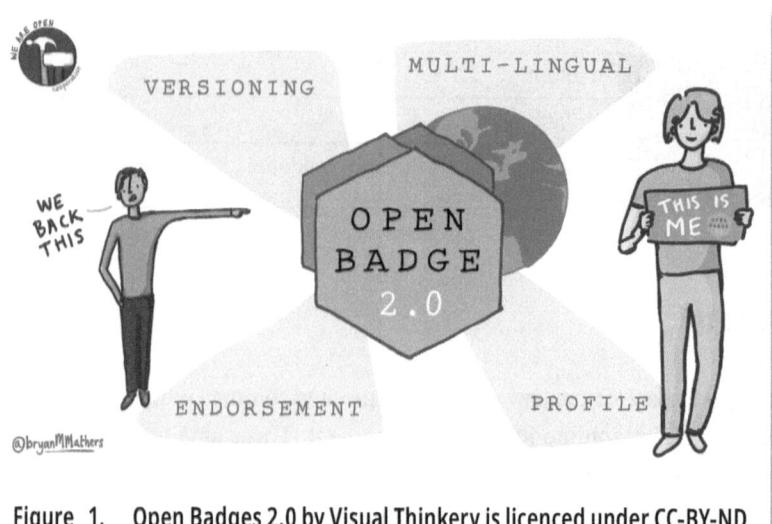

Figure 1.   Open Badges 2.0 by Visual Thinkery is licenced under CC-BY-ND

Example

Language acquisition is a complex, often lengthy journey. Much of our international communication today is mediated through technological environments such as messenger services, social media channels, and virtual rooms. Skills in computer-mediated communication can be acquired through engagement with virtual exchange, defined by the Erasmus Plus-funded EVOLVE project as:

> " sustained, technology-enabled, people-to-people education programmes or activities in which constructive communication and interaction takes place between individuals or groups who are geographically separated and/or from different cultural backgrounds, with the support of educators or facilitators" (https://evolve-erasmus.eu/about-evolve/what-is-virtual-exchange/).

The deployment of open badges issued at specified points in a learning arc (Cross & Galley, 2012), can help build awareness of these steps to competence. In their investigation of the Clavier virtual exchange, Hauck and MacKinnon (2016) identified a framework for the design and implementation of open badges in virtual exchange activities. Including badges as part of course design offers an opportunity to critically review learning design assumptions and to communicate the intended learning outcomes to participants. Once awarded, badges are owned and managed by the learner who is able to include them in their own online presence.

Largely as a result of the research into Clavier's use of open badges in language learning through virtual exchange, open badges were implemented in The Erasmus+ Virtual Exchange initiative which began in 2018 with support from the European Commission (https://europa.eu/youth/erasmusvirtual). This multi-partner initiative aims to mainstream the use of virtual exchange in order to increase the number of young people who experience intercultural dialogue. The open badges provide a mechanism for raising awareness of online presence and communicating connections fostered between European, Middle Eastern, and North African regions. The role of the open badges was chiefly to act as signifiers of activity completion which could then be shared online to build and connect a network of expertise in virtual exchange. One of the partners, UNICollaboration, was responsible for the procurement and management of a suitable open badge platform for all activities using *Open Badge Factory*. UNICollaboration designs and delivers training in virtual exchange, known as Transnational Exchange Projects (TEPs), for practitioners in higher education institutions and for youth workers, providing professional development and building capacity for virtual exchange. UNICollaboration connects language educators who are already involved in virtual exchange with practitioners in other disciplines where their understanding of linguistic and intercultural issues may facilitate successful interactions across national and disciplinary boundaries, leading to groundbreaking new collaborations. To date the Erasmus+ Virtual Exchange initiative has issued about 12,000 open badges for activity completion and an ecosystem of meta- and micro – level skills is communicated on the Erasmus+ Virtual Exchange Youth hub.

Chapter 9. Open badges

Benefits

Open badge use is technically quite straightforward and helps learning designers draw attention to what they value. Reflecting on how and when a badge is awarded and setting criteria for that award are useful processes to incorporate into learning design. Deploying digital micro-credentials when the learning activity is delivered online furthers the acquisition of digital skills and creates the potential for learner curation of an online professional presence. Open badges are more secure than paper certificates as they carry data which tracks back to the issuer and the reason for issue and cannot easily be falsified. Use of open badges fits well with the creation and sharing of a reflective e-portfolio, encouraging engagement with deeper learning practice.

Potential issues

It is still quite early days for the use of open badges and therefore many may be unaware of their significance. This can be addressed with good communication around how to collect and display a badge. Designing for use of open badges may take time and experimentation, preferably in consultation with the badge recipients. However, adopting an inclusive approach to the implementation of badges does offer a real opportunity to reconnect learners to curriculum design and thus strengthen their engagement. An example of this could be the use of open badges aligned with UNESCO's sustainable development goals.

Looking to the future

> Including open badges in learning design can bring an element of gamification to formal learning and, when shared and displayed, can help connect badge earners to new learning opportunities through display portals such as *Open Badge Passport*. There are examples of badge applications internationally such as the *Badgeons la Normandie* project, which increase access to learning across formal and informal settings. Such examples may be particularly relevant

> to language learning given the reduction in access to language learning in formal education due to barriers of cost and time that many experience.

References

Cross, S., & Galley, R. (2012). *MOOC badging and the learning arc* [blog post]. http://oro.open.ac.uk/42038/

HASTAC. (2020). *Digital badges*. https://www.hastac.org/initiatives/digital-badges#projects

Hauck, M., & MacKinnon, T. (2016). A new approach to assessing online intercultural exchange: soft certification of participant engagement. In R. O'Dowd & T. Lewis (Eds), *Online intercultural exchange: policy, pedagogy, practice*. Routledge. https://doi.org/10.4324/9781315678931

MacArthur Foundation. (2012, March 3). *Badges for lifelong learning competition: winners announced*. https://www.macfound.org/press/press-releases/badges-lifelong-learning-competition-winners-announced/

Resources

Badge wiki: a comprehensive collection of resources on open badges: https://badge.wiki/wiki/Main_Page

Badgeons la Normandie project: https://misterppqx.name/bln/le-projet-badgeons-la-normandie/

Erasmus Plus Virtual Exchange digital badges: https://youtu.be/Hq5BE-hoEKA

O'Dowd, R., & Lewis, T. (2016). (Eds). *Online intercultural exchange: policy, pedagogy, practice*. Routledge. https://doi.org/10.4324/9781315678931

Open Badge Passport: https://openbadgepassport.com/

Research into the use of open badges: a curation of publications: https://badge.wiki/wiki/Research

What is an open badge?: https://youtu.be/Xc4xDgNbl6Y

What is virtual exchange?: https://en.wikipedia.org/wiki/Virtual_exchange

Why badges?: https://badge.wiki/wiki/Why_Badges%3F

Comparative judgement
assess student production without absolute judgements

Josh Sumner[1]

Potential impact	medium
Timescale	medium term
Keywords	comparative judgement, assessment, reliability

What is it?

Comparative Judgement (CJ) has emerged as a technique that typically makes use of holistic judgement to assess difficult-to-specify constructs such as production (speaking and writing) in Modern Foreign Languages (MFL). In traditional approaches, markers assess candidates' work one-by-one in an absolute manner, assigning scores to different elements (analytic marking). In CJ, however, markers compare two pieces and consider the overall merits of each. They make one binary, holistic judgement as to which is better. This approach exploits humans' natural ability to compare; we find it easy, for example, to say which of two people is taller, but struggle to give precise estimates of height.

By using a collection of 'paired comparisons', in which items are judged several times, a rank order from 'worst' to 'best' is produced. Properties such as overall consistency of judgement can be evaluated, as can difficult-to-rate items or unreliable assessors.

Technology facilitates implementation of CJ: work is uploaded to web-based software. Multiple markers ('judges') make comparisons of two pieces of work presented side-by-side. Software using adaptive CJ, involving 'rounds'

---

1. Dean Close School, Cheltenham, United Kingdom; jma.sumner@gmail.com; https://orcid.org/0000-0002-5490-9266

How to cite: Sumner, J. (2021). Comparative judgement: assess student production without absolute judgements. In T. Beaven & F. Rosell-Aguilar (Eds), *Innovative language pedagogy report* (pp. 63-67). Research-publishing.net. https://doi.org/10.14705/rpnet.2021.50.1237

of marking of work increasingly similar in quality, requires fewer comparisons but produces arguably equally reliable rank orders. CJ has proven reliable in assessment of first language, mathematical problem-solving, and written work in humanities. Findings include a higher level of inter- and intra-assessor reliability compared to traditional assessment, though research into application in MFL is limited; Pollitt and Murray's (1993) small-scale study concentrated on foreign language speaking, and there have been trials in some UK schools.

As research has found that 23% of students candidates receive the 'wrong' grade at General Certificate of Secondary Education (GCSE) in MFL using traditional techniques (Rhead, Black, & de Moira, 2018, p. 17), teachers, school leaders, and examination boards may consider eschewing analytic marking using criterion-based mark schemes in favour of holistic CJs.

Example

The MFL department at Sandringham Research School (2018) trialled CJ using the software *No More Marking* (www.nomoremarking.com) to assess writing in end-of-year exams. Teachers were presented with pieces of two anonymised students' work – both their own and others' – on screen side-by-side, and judged which was overall 'better'. The same piece of work was judged numerous times, by different teachers; through different comparisons, an algorithm brought together all judgements, providing a rank order. The department found a reliability metric of 0.89 and that student work was quicker to assess, though could not be used to give individual feedback.

In future, the introduction of pre-marked items into comparisons, 'anchor responses', could allow grades to be assigned using norm-referencing. This technique could be used by examination boards.

Benefits

With CJ, there is no change to the preparation or administration of tasks, only to assessment, but its benefits are numerous.

CJ saves time; judges make one judgement rather than numerous ones against different criteria. This replicates the natural process of reading and is faster. Higher reliability is achieved without needing time-consuming moderation.

Used across a department, as part of the process teachers see not only the work of their own class, but a range of student responses, without requiring judgement on the reliability of colleagues' marking as in a moderation. CJ thus has a formative perspective for teachers.

CJ does not require elaboration of mark schemes prior to a test, nor in a 'standardisation' process. 'Unpredictable' responses are more easily dealt with, and teachers may find students produce more novel, ambitious responses; traditional marking may stymie linguistic development and limit creativity as students are concerned with 'jumping through hoops'. CJ exploits teachers' expert knowledge and professional competency of 'good' production without demanding it be tightly defined.

CJ allows for a more accurate ranking order by avoiding markers using the middle of any level-based rubric, precluding the 'bunching' of marks due to reluctance to give zero or full marks. Determination of a rank order is more accurate than with criterion-based marking and inter-assessor reliability is higher due to repeated comparisons.

Potential issues

CJ is only suitable for summative assessment. Analytic scales provide feedback to students and teachers regarding relative strengths and weaknesses. A position in a ranking order, or a score, gives no information regarding learning, nor how to improve. Teachers wanting to use a task assessed through CJ formatively may need to mark work again analytically. However, subsequent instruction could be improved by teachers' knowledge of a cohort's performance. Examination boards may be reluctant to adopt CJ. The relativistic approach makes it difficult to appeal marks; the basis of assessment is a series of comparisons by numerous examiners, not transparent scores given by one.

Use of holistic judgement precludes weighting of elements of production (e.g. communication is weighted more highly than accuracy at GCSE). Markers may be swayed by salient features, such as inaccuracy of spelling. In addition, implementation of CJ for speaking is problematic, as it relies on memory; two audio files can only be subsequently rather than concurrently compared, unlike writing.

Furthermore, the absence of prescriptive mark schemes, hailed as a benefit, may only work for so long. Research into use of CJ in Geography found examiners used mark schemes implicitly due to knowledge of criteria of traditional approaches: a shared construct existed in an established community of practice through familiarity with extant methods.

Looking to the future

> The issues involved in using CJ to assess MFL production are much like those involved in assessing other complex constructs, and studies into its use for these have been positive. There is nothing, in my opinion, that makes MFL production, particularly writing, a wildly different construct. Consideration of implementation of CJ is crucial, lest we resign ourselves to the unreliability of current assessment. Examination boards could consider its use in high-stakes assessment, and schools could employ it to produce more reliable internal assessments which also save teachers time.

References

Pollitt, A., & Murray, N. L. (1993). What raters really pay attention to. *Studies in language testing, 3,* 74-91.

Rhead, S., Black, B., & de Moira, A. (2018). *Marking consistency metrics: an update.* Ofqual.

Sandringham Research School. (2018, December 7). Comparative judgement: a workshop exploring its use in MFL. *Sandringham Research School Blog*. https://researchschool.org.uk/sandringham/news/comparative-judgement-a-workshop-exploring-its-use-in-mfl/

Resources

Christodoulou, D. (2016). *Making good progress? The future of assessment for learning*. Oxford University Press.

Christodoulou, D. (2018). Comparative judgement – the next big revolution in assessment? *ResearchEd, 1*, 13-14.

Pollitt, A. (2012). The method of adaptive comparative judgement. *Assessment in education: principles, policy and practice*, 19(3), 281-300. https://doi.org/10.1080/0969594x.2012.665354

Stock, P. (2017). Compare the marking: using comparative judgement to assess student progress at secondary level. *Impact, 1*, 12-15.

Oxford Education. (2019). *What is comparative judgement?* https://youtu.be/KLVtvBPXQ2U

If you want to try a simple comparative judgement experiment, you might enjoy doing this activity: https://www.nomoremarking.com/demo2

Technology-facilitated oral homework
leveraging technology to get students speaking outside the classroom

David Shanks[1]

Potential impact	medium
Timescale	medium term
Keywords	technology-facilitated oral homework, speaking, recording, foreign language anxiety, homework, low stakes

What is it?

Technology-Facilitated Oral Homework (TFOH) is an umbrella term for the use of digital technologies that enable learners to record themselves speaking the target language and submit recordings to their teachers from outside the formal classroom environment.

It is understandable why speaking and pronunciation work might fall by the wayside in some language learning contexts. Limited classroom contact time, pressure to cover curriculum content, high student-to-teacher ratios, challenges in monitoring speaking activities, and the need for one-to-one time for effective oral assessment are just some of the reasons why oral work might drop down the priority list. Peer pressure and Foreign Language Anxiety (FLA) can also make speaking the target language a daunting prospect for students. To compound matters, homework in our subject has traditionally focused predominantly upon the written word. Limited in-lesson opportunities to practise orally and little-to-no chance to do so between formal lessons could leave some students lacking

1. Harris Federation, Croydon, United Kingdom; david.shanks@harrisfederation.org.uk

How to cite: Shanks, D. (2021). Technology-facilitated oral homework: leveraging technology to get students speaking outside the classroom. In T. Beaven & F. Rosell-Aguilar (Eds), *Innovative language pedagogy report* (pp. 69-75). Research-publishing.net. https://doi.org/10.14705/rpnet.2021.50.1238

in oral confidence, with low levels of L2 decoding ability and low levels of motivation for language learning more generally.

TFOH is an approach that aims to overcome some of these common challenges and develop students' oral confidences by providing additional opportunities for practising in a 'lower stakes', self-regulated environment. The goal is that this practice could lead to a decrease in debilitative FLA, as well as increases in students' oral confidences, L2 decoding abilities, and motivation.

TFOH does not currently appear to be a widespread practice at the secondary school level. The research base is also limited, and focuses on adult learners in higher education settings (e.g. Correa & Grim, 2014; Guanoluisa, 2017; Méndez, 2010). The proliferation of Internet-connected mobile devices over the last decade and the concurrent emergence of more affordable, user-friendly digital technologies (that include audio and video recording facilities), however, mean that TFOH is becoming an increasingly viable option for a wider range of settings.

Example

As part of their French course, a class of Year 9 (13-14 years old) students in London, UK took part in 'Let's Talk Homework', a case study involving an intervention of five TFOH tasks (Shanks, 2018). In place of their usual weekly written or learning homework, students were assigned a TFOH task, in response to which they recorded and uploaded an audio file to a private online bulletin board set up and managed by their teacher through a free Padlet account (see Figure 1). Task types were varied in structure and focus. Read-aloud activities invited students to practise sound-symbol correspondences and develop confidence in pronunciation. More extended tasks invited students to create language themselves, for example, by describing a photograph.

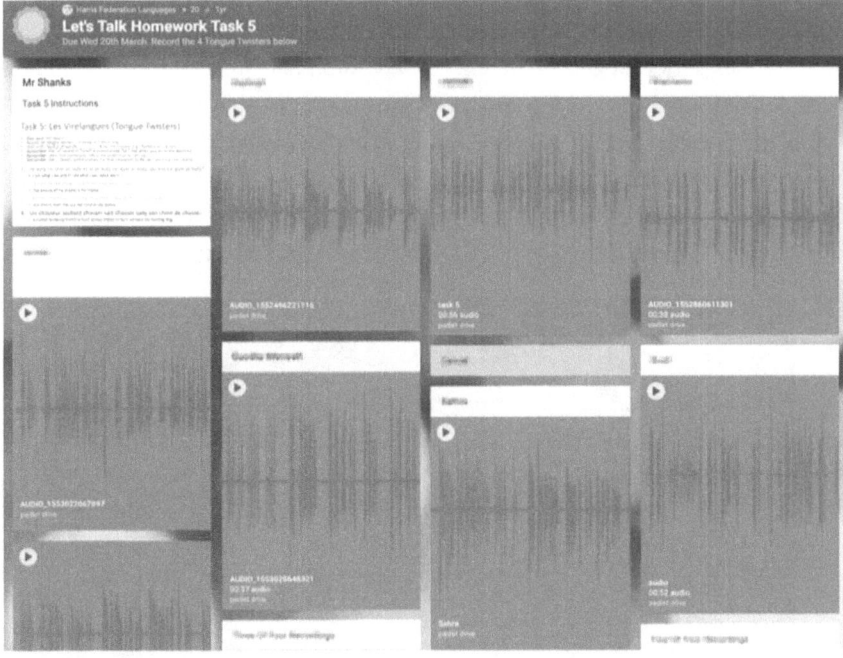

Figure 1. Students' audio responses posted to the teacher's online Padlet bulletin board

All students managed to submit audio, with the vast majority submitting directly through the free Padlet app from a mobile device. A small number of students uploaded a link to an audio file recorded via another method, such as their mobile phone's native voice recorder app or the recording app *Vocaroo*. That the case study took place successfully in a state school with above national levels of socio-economic disadvantage is encouraging in terms of the feasibility of using TFOH in a wider range of contexts. Many other websites, apps, or digital tools can be used to run TFOH, and there are pockets of innovative practice being shared online, for example through the #MFLTwitterati and #MFLChat networks.

Benefits

The main benefit of TFOH is that it allows students increased opportunities to practise orally – something any language teacher would want for their students. It can let students more regularly go through the important and confidence-building process of physically producing new target language sounds, words, and sentences. TFOH can provide a safer, lower-stakes environment in which to practise, away from the peer pressure of classmates and the teacher. In the 'Let's Talk Homework' case study, it became clear that TFOH can provide a space for students to monitor their own oral performance and self-regulate their learning at their own speed:

> "I recorded my voice once to listen to how I did it and then I didn't post it, because I just practised it and then I did it again" (Student 14).

> "I first say it in front of my sister to see how I sound then I try and record, and if I don't like how I sound I'll delete it, and just keep on doing that until I'm actually happy with what I recorded" (Student 3).

> "for the tongue twisters I had to record like ten different times" (Student 13).

The teacher involved in the same case study also observed that TFOH can have a positive impact upon oral confidence, pronunciation, and anxiety reduction:

> "In class, they [two particular students] are much more forthcoming […] that reluctance to speak was linked to not knowing how to pronounce things […] and a lack of confidence about just giving things a go. [They…] have started really speaking a lot more confidently and a lot more willingly in class […] being able to record without an audience definitely helped anxiety".

Potential issues

Whilst conversation-like tasks are currently possible (e.g. by the teacher recording sequences of questions or using *Qwiqr*'s conversation feature), the currently asynchronous nature of TFOH means that it is not yet possible to replicate elements of spontaneity, listenership, and support in the ways that are possible with authentic face-to-face oral practice. It is also important to consider equality of access to the requisite technology, especially when working with schools that serve socio-economically disadvantaged students. Support or providing alternative ways of completing TFOH could be considered, e.g. morning or after-school homework clubs with hardware access, use of a shared class devices, signposting to the library or computer room facilities, suggesting use of a parent's or sibling's phone, placing files on the school's student file server, or changing the app or method of submission used. Time, expertise, and support needs to be available for helping teachers and students develop the technological knowledge of the digital tools required in each context.

Looking to the future

There is an increasing number of digital tools that can be used for TFOH. As such, TFOH could realistically become a much more widely used type of homework task, used regularly by language teachers. TFOH will likely be most effective when the tasks are carefully designed, embedded regularly within courses, and are accompanied by feedback to support learners.

We increasingly interact orally with technology through Intelligent Virtual Assistants such as *Siri*, *Cortana*, and *Alexa* (see Underwood, this volume). Similar voice recognition and artificially intelligent technologies could be put to use in language learning contexts. It is possible to imagine increasingly complex oral human-machine interactions that soon resemble real conversations, with the appropriate machine responses based upon the learner's voice input guiding the learning conversations. Analysis of the learner's

> performance, automated feedback, and remedial tasks could also be integrated into such interactions. Google's "Human-like Open-Domain Chatbot" *Meena* is already providing interesting insights into this area.

References

Correa, M., & Grim, F. (2014). Audio recordings as a self-awareness tool for improving second language pronunciation in the phonetics and phonology classroom: sample activities. *Currents in Teaching & Learning*, *6*(2). https://www.worcester.edu/WorkArea/DownloadAsset.aspx?id=5376

Guanoluisa, F. C. (2017). Influence of oral homework on oral competence in a beginning English class at Technical University of Cotopaxi. *UTCiencia, Ciencia y Tecnología al servicio del pueblo*, *2*(3), 162-169. http://investigacion.utc.edu.ec/revistasutc/index.php/utciencia/article/view/36/37

Méndez, E. (2010). How to set up oral homework: a case of limited technology. *English Teaching Forum*, *48*(3), 10-19).

Shanks, D. M. (2018). *Let's talk homework: a case study of how an intervention of TFOH tasks impacts upon Year 9 students' motivation in French*. MA Dissertation. King's College London. https://www.dropbox.com/s/rk4rqt37ez96tvf/1581025%20Dissertation%20April%202019%20David%20Shanks.pdf?dl=0

Underwood, J. (2021). Speaking to machines: motivating speaking through oral interaction with intelligent assistants. In T. Beaven & F. Rosell-Aguilar (Eds), *Innovative language pedagogy report* (pp. 127-132). Research-publishing.net. https://doi.org/10.14705/rpnet.2021.50.1247

Resources

#MFLChat thread on TFOH: http://learninglinguist.co.uk/mflchat-teaching-speaking-and-listening-remotely-27-04-20/

National Centre for Excellence for Language Pedagogy – Oral Homework: https://resources.ncelp.org/concern/resources/6m311p430?locale=en

List of TFOH digital tools:
Flipgrid: https://flipgrid.com/
Lingt: https://lingt.com/
Online-voice-recorder: https://online-voice-recorder.com/
Padlet: https://padlet.com/
Qwikr: https://qwiqr.education
Showbie: https://showbie.com
Vocaroo: https://vocaroo.com/

Ipsative assessment
measuring personal improvement

Antonio Martínez-Arboleda[1]

Potential impact	low
Timescale	long term
Keywords	assessment, feedback, feedforward, learning gain, value-added

What is it?

Ipsative assessment is an approach to evaluating student progress that covers a wide range of assessment and feedback practices. It has been around since 1944, but its fully-fledged implementation into formal education, including in the field of language teaching and learning, is still in its infancy.

The word 'ipsative' comes from Latin *ipse, -a, -um*, which means 'self'. This gives us an indication of the meaning of ipsative assessment in education: the evaluation of the quality of the performance of a student by reference to their previous performance(s), not by reference to the rest of the cohort (norm-referenced assessment), nor against expected standards based on programme objectives (criterion-referenced assessment). The term ipsative assessment is also used in human resources and psychometric testing, but with a different meaning, to refer to tests where respondents have to select their preferred option out of two or more available ones.

In ipsative assessment, students receive an indication of their achievement that represents the extent of their improvements from their previous assessed task(s)

---

1. University of Leeds, Leeds, United Kingdom; a.martinez-arboleda@leeds.ac.uk; https://orcid.org/0000-0002-4391-5417

How to cite: Martínez-Arboleda, A. (2021). Ipsative assessment: measuring personal improvement. In T. Beaven & F. Rosell-Aguilar (Eds), *Innovative language pedagogy report* (pp. 77-82). Research-publishing.net. https://doi.org/10.14705/rpnet.2021.50.1239

Chapter 12. Ipsative assessment

in relation to one or more objectives. In turn, ipsative feedback (formal self-referential feedback) describes and celebrates those specific improvements, identifies areas lacking in progress, and proposes feedforward.

Ideally, in ipsative assessment, criterion-referenced grades are not calculated or communicated and, if so, they are kept in the background as a secondary indicator. As for norm-referenced criteria, these are simply incompatible with the spirit of ipsative assessment. Learning gain, the distance between two points in time in a learning journey, is a critical concept in ipsative assessment, but one that deserves problematisation: is it really about the distance travelled, which inevitably leads us to numerical figures (ipsative grading), or is it more about narrating and evaluating the details of a journey that is much richer than the miles it covered (ipsative feedback)?

Example

The delivery of effective ipsative feedback in languages should incorporate tangible comparisons and reflections on at least two different performances throughout a period of time. However, digesting this feedback, typically presented in a combination of annotations to the pieces of work and feedback forms, can be a challenge for students. In addition, contextualising feedback and feedforward comments in tasks that are embodied in formats such as video or websites can be rather tedious and ineffective when using traditional written forms of feedback.

However, thanks to audio-visual feedback, using video feedback tools, such as *Screencast-O-Matic*, language teachers can incorporate the principles of ipsative assessment seamlessly into their feedback. The technology allows the teacher to bring up and visualise two pieces of work on one screen, regardless of their format, point at different parts of both tasks and record the oral comments with the visual indications on both pieces of work, using any other supporting images or resources. Providing oral feedback with visual support is becoming a new approach that can easily break with the cultural conventions of criterion-referenced regimes, allowing the teacher to set the new rules of the ipsative game.

Ipsative feedback should not be used to communicate or justify criterion-referenced marks, but rather to discuss progress in tasks and ways to improve. When numerical marks for a task are required by regulations, there is nothing preventing teachers from releasing any developmental feedback a few days before the mark. That way, a feedforward space for reflection-action is created. At the end of the day, providing feedback is an essential element of teaching, whereas grading should be seen as a more collegial and administrative process that requires other sorts of checks and balances, as they are integral to the awarding powers of the institution (Martínez-Arboleda, 2018). This pedagogy has been introduced experimentally, although under the umbrella of the technology that empowers it, at the University of Leeds (Figure 1).

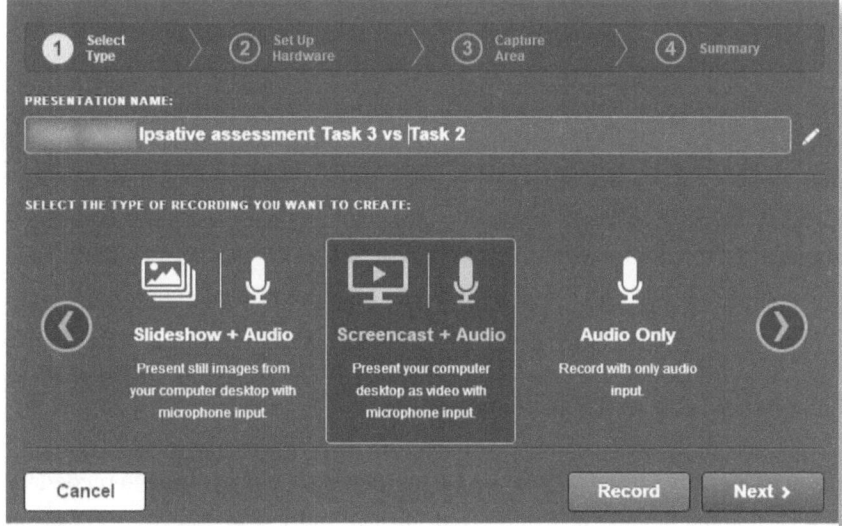

Figure 1. The Mediasite Desktop Capture tool used to provide audio-visual feedback at the University of Leeds

Benefits

For Rattray (2018), ipsative approaches and spaces help learners develop, in a safe manner, "resilience, optimism and hope" (p. 101). These are particularly

Chapter 12. Ipsative assessment

important affective attributes in such a performative, personal, emotional, and socially outlooking experience as language learning because the learner is not under pressure to meet externally set standards. Moreover, meta-learning and self-reflection are consubstantial to ipsative feedback. For most authors, ipsative assessment improves learner motivation. This is particularly important for students who require additional support, distance learners, and self-directed learning.

Ipsative approaches are ideal for those practitioners who believe that feedback, as an act of learning support, and criterion-referenced assessment, are two completely different operations which can interfere with each other, both in nature and purpose. For Hughes (2011), the latter places the emphasis on reliability, consistency, and fixed goals that may be out of reach for some learners at the expense of personalised evaluations of incremental progress.

Ideologically and culturally, ipsative assessment is a pedagogically sound response to the alienating consequences of both neoliberal competition-fuelled modes of human relations (Rattray, 2018) and more traditional forms of social control exercised through numerical academic grading (Martínez-Arboleda, 2016). Some of the specific benefits include the introduction of (1) more usable feedback that refers closely to the current performance, (2) task-oriented feedforward, and (3) the closing of the feedback loop. All the above would, according to Hughes (2011), contribute to addressing the shortcomings of criteria-driven assessment regimes.

A form of ipsative assessment for language learning is already used in secondary schools in some countries. Tutors keep track of individual student progression across standardised grades, setting targets, motivating students, and working towards the achievement of higher grades. The best-known indicator in the UK is called 'Progress 8'.

> "It aims to capture the progress a pupil makes from the end of primary school to the end of secondary school. It is a type of value-added measure, which means that pupils' results are compared to the

> actual achievements of other pupils with similar prior attainment" (Progress 8, 2016, p. 2).

Despite the merits of progress indicators used in schools, in most educational systems what really seems to matter socially, sadly, is the actual grade achieved at the end, not the speed or the length of the progress. In this context, it is the educators' role to promote, as much as they can, a change of culture within the current institutional and professional boundaries.

Potential issues

For ipsative assessment to be effective, the design of the assessed tasks has to be approached as part of an assessment plan whose components span strategically throughout the year, or even through a whole qualification. The successive tasks need to contain threads that allow for diachronic and personalised comparison. Relatively open-ended assessed tasks offer more flexibility. Ipsative assessment requires a careful refining of tasks for levels above B1 of the Common European Framework of Reference (CEFR), where students can frequently experience a learning plateau effect. Finally, students need to be educated in the process and art of identifying quality (Sadler, 2010). Telling them what is wrong and what is right with their work is not sufficient.

Looking to the future

> In formal education, 'ipsativity' will be facilitated by new interfaces and tools enabling tutors to access the feedback history of each student in their virtual learning environment in order to compare consecutive tasks. Learning management systems allow for personalised paths punctuated with tasks, as well as for a very granular, often automatised, monitoring of engagement and performance. This can facilitate teachers' ipsative endeavours. Portfolios of learning, which are well embedded in our discipline, can be given a greater role as part of an ipsative transformation.

References

Hughes, G. (2011). Towards a personal best: a case for introducing ipsative assessment in higher education. *Studies in Higher Education, 36*(3), 353-367. https://doi.org/10.1080/0 3075079.2010.486859

Martínez-Arboleda, A. (2016). Historia oral digital: reprogramación y empoderamiento educativo y social. In J. A. Bresciano & F. Sossai (Eds), *El conocimiento histórico en el ciberespacio: prácticas académicas y proyección social*. Ediciones Cruz del Sur.

Martínez-Arboleda, A. (2018). Audiovisual student feedback (ASF) in higher education: teaching and power. *The International Journal of E-Learning and Educational Technologies in the Digital Media (IJEETDM), 4*(4), 98-113. https://doi.org/10.17781/ p002544

Progress 8. (2016). *How Progress 8 and Attainment 8 measures are calculated*. Department for Education. https://assets.publishing.service.gov.uk/government/uploads/system/ uploads/attachment_data/file/561021/Progress_8_and_Attainment_8_how_measures_ are_calculated.pdf

Rattray, J. (2018). Affect and ipsative approaches as a counter to pedagogic frailty: the guardian of traditional models of student success. *Higher Education Research & Development, 37*(7), 1489-1500. https://doi.org/10.1080/07294360.2018.1494141

Sadler, D. R. (2010). Beyond feedback: developing student capability in complex appraisal. *Assessment & Evaluation in Higher Education, 35*(5), 535-550. https://doi. org/10.1080/02602930903541015

Resources

Hughes, G. (2017). *Ipsative assessment and personal learning gain*. Palgrave Macmillan.

Hughes, G. (2014, December 9). Want to help students improve their work? Mark them on their progress. *The Guardian*. https://www.theguardian.com/higher-education-network/2014/ dec/09/mark-students-progress-ipsative-assessment

Penn, P. R., & Wells, I. G. (2018). Making assessment promote effective learning practices: an example of ipsative assessment from the school of psychology at UEL. *Psychology Teaching Review, 24*(2), 70-74.

The translation turn
a communicative approach to translation in the language classroom

Ángeles Carreres[1] and María Noriega-Sánchez[2]

Potential impact	medium
Timescale	ongoing
Keywords	translation, translation in language teaching and learning, linguistic mediation, pedagogical translation

What is it?

Translation, explicitly or implicitly, has been a constant presence in the teaching and learning of languages throughout the ages. It may therefore seem surprising that it should find a place in a report on innovative pedagogies. While translation has indeed been used for centuries for the purpose of language learning, there is no doubt that recent approaches in the area of language and translation pedagogy have helped re-conceptualise – and re-operationalise – translation in radically new ways.

For decades, translation had been identified with the grammar translation method, and decried as incompatible with a communicative approach. In the last two decades, however, we have seen a thorough re-examination of the role of translation in language teaching and learning. A range of factors have contributed to this trend, among them, the questioning of the monolingual principle in language pedagogy, extensive developments in the area of audiovisual translation, exciting innovations in the field of professional translation didactics,

---

1. University of Cambridge, Cambridge, United Kingdom; ac289@cam.ac.uk

2. University of Cambridge, Cambridge, United Kingdom; mn316@cam.ac.uk

How to cite: Carreres, Á., & Noriega-Sánchez, M. (2021). The translation turn: a communicative approach to translation in the language classroom. In T. Beaven & F. Rosell-Aguilar (Eds), *Innovative language pedagogy report* (pp. 83-89). Research-publishing.net. https://doi.org/10.14705/rpnet.2021.50.1240

the huge success of translation-based digital platforms such as Duolingo, and, crucially, the introduction of the notion of mediation in the Common European Framework of Reference for languages (CEFR, 2001), later expanded in the *Companion volume* (CEFR, 2018).

A key feature of recent approaches is the emphasis on translation as a real-world communicative activity. As such, translation is seen not only – sometimes not even primarily – as a useful tool to enhance linguistic competence, but as a key skill (a language activity, to follow the CEFR) to be developed by any language learner, not just by those planning to enter careers as professional translators. Therefore, translation is increasingly regarded not just as a means, but also, crucially, as an end in itself in second language education. This shift has led some to suggest that we have entered a *translation turn* in language pedagogy.

The introduction of the notion of mediation in the CEFR has provided a basis for normalising the use of translation in language learning. Under the label of linguistic mediation, the CEFR includes all those language activities aimed at enabling communication between people when it is faced with obstacles that stand in its way (CEFR, 2001, p. 14). One of these possible obstacles is the absence of a common language. So, as described in the CEFR, mediation includes – but is not limited to – translation and interpreting. With its emphasis on the language learner as a social agent (action-oriented approach), the CEFR sees the development of plurilingual and pluricultural competence as a key objective of language learning.

Yet the CEFR in its 2001 edition did not quite follow through on its endorsement of mediation and translation in that it did not offer detailed descriptors to describe mediating competence at each of the levels (A1, A2, B1, etc.). This has been rectified in the *Companion volume with new descriptors*, published in 2018. As well as providing descriptors for mediation, the *Companion volume* places increased emphasis on the development of the learner's plurilingual competence, thus strengthening the position of translation within the CEFR.

Examples

We briefly outline here a few examples of translation tasks that aim to help learners improve their language skills through translation and develop their translation skills, particularly in regards to translation into the L2, but also more generally. They can be adapted to different educational contexts and levels of linguistic competence. The focus is on translation as a communicative activity. Where appropriate, skills are practised in an integrated manner, with opportunities to develop listening and oral skills, as well as writing and reading, and through the use of various media (written texts, films, plays, audios, images).

Task design is guided by a learner-centred approach, and pair work and group work are used to foster collaboration. Real-world translation tasks with clear briefs (e.g. translating a *TED Talk*) are combined with more controlled activities. Awareness-raising activities are also important to get learners to reflect on the translation process. For reasons of space, the following is a succinct list of suggested tasks, but they are envisaged as part of didactic sequences with scaffolding.

- Audiovisual translation activities: intralinguistic and interlinguistic subtitling, and dubbing of films; voiceover of documentaries; audio description for the blind and visually impaired (translation of images into words).

- Working with parallel texts in L1 and L2, using recipes, formal letters, contracts, etc. to identify text types, formulaic expressions, and stylistic features.

- Translating ads (wordplay, puns) and political speeches (rhetorical features) with a focus on persuasive language.

- Interpreting from L1 into L2: role-plays in which students carry out dialogues for real-life situations (e.g. hospital interpreter, tourist guide, etc.).

Chapter 13. The translation turn

- Back-translation: students are given two translations of the same text and have to reconstruct, in pairs, the source text to identify issues to do with linguistic choices and stylistic nuance. They are then given the source text, and a discussion on translation strategies and techniques follows.

- Translating plays: focus on oral and pragmatic features, as well as the challenges of translating for the stage. Students translate a scene and film themselves acting it out.

- Translating comics and graphic novels: constraints of text and image, cultural references, phonic features (onomatopoeias, interjections). Working with poetry can also be productive in analysing phonic aspects (rhyme, alliteration).

- Group projects: collaborative translation using shared documents (discussing choices and negotiating a final version), translating for non-governmental organisations, etc.

- Individual portfolios: compiling own translations and reflecting on progress; using and assessing new technologies (linguistic corpora, glossaries, automatic translators, etc.).

Benefits

In today's multicultural and multilingual societies, the ability to mediate between speakers of different languages is an increasingly vital skill. Through translation-based activities, learners can:

- develop their plurilingual and pluricultural competences;
- enhance their contrastive awareness of both the source and target language;
- engage with a variety of media;

- develop awareness of genre and text type;
- sharpen their understanding of grammar;
- broaden their lexical knowledge;
- develop stylistic awareness;
- develop dictionary and documentation skills;
- acquire know-how in the use of translation technologies;
- enhance their creativity, critical thinking, and problem solving; and
- gain autonomy as learners.

Potential issues

With translation now being an element in the school language curriculum at General Certificate of Secondary Education (GCSE), AS and A Level in the UK, opportunities open up to utilise its motivational and learning potential with young learners. However, implementation also poses significant challenges. The constraints imposed by current assessment methods and the lack of specific teacher training have often resulted in pedagogical and testing practices that hark back to the grammar translation method and risk doing more harm than good.

Beyond the UK secondary context, assessment presents a more general challenge. If we want to move away from outdated notions of translation as a near-mechanical transfer of meaning, we will need to explore more holistic evaluation methods that encourage a more realistic, creative, and socially relevant view of translation. A narrow focus on grammatical accuracy and dictionary knowledge may be indicated in certain contexts, but it must be balanced with more authentic translation activities.

A further challenge – but also an exciting opportunity – is posed by the increasing multilingual make-up of many classrooms throughout all stages of education. The fact that learners often do not share the same L1 and L2 means that traditional notions of directionality in translation pedagogy need to be rethought. At the same time, multilingual groups present the chance to introduce new classroom dynamics that can be empowering and enriching for learners.

Chapter 13. The translation turn

Looking to the future

> While there is now growing consensus favouring the use of translation for language learning, much work remains to be done on the design and implementation of translation-based activities in the classroom, as well as on assessment.
>
> The focus on plurilingual competence in the CEFR and in the field more generally has been a factor in the reinstatement of translation. At the same time, however, if translation is to deploy its full potential in this regard, researchers and practitioners are going to have to think creatively and adapt to the demands of increasingly multilingual classrooms. We will no doubt see pedagogical proposals responding to this new paradigm in the coming months and years.

References

CEFR. (2001). *Common European framework of reference for languages: learning, teaching, assessment*. Cambridge University Press. https://rm.coe.int/1680459f97

CEFR. (2018). *Common European framework of reference for languages: learning, teaching, assessment. Companion volume with new descriptors*. Council of Europe. https://rm.coe.int/cefr-companion-volume-with-new-descriptors-2018/1680787989

Resources

Carreres, Á. (2014). Translation as a means and as an end: reassessing the divide. *The Interpreter and Translator Trainer, 8*(3), 123-135. https://doi.org/10.1080/1750399X.2014.908561

Carreres, Á., Noriega-Sánchez, M., & Calduch, C. (2018). *Mundos en palabras: learning advanced Spanish through translation*. Routledge. https://www.routledge.com/Mundos-en-palabras-Learning-Advanced-Spanish-through-Translation/Carreres-Noriega-Sanchez-Calduch/p/book/9780415695374

González-Davies, M. (2004). *Multiple voices in the translation classroom*. John Benjamins.

Laviosa, S., & Gonzáles-Davies, M. (2020). (Eds). *The Routledge handbook of translation and education*. Routledge.

Pintado Gutiérrez, L. (2019). Mapping translation in foreign language teaching: demystifying the construct. In M. Koletnik & N. Frœliger (Eds), *Translation and language teaching: continuing the dialogue* (pp. 23-38). Cambridge Scholars Publishing.

Clipflair, a platform for foreign language learning through interactive revoicing and captioning of clips: http://www.clipflair.net/

PluriTAV, a learning platform for English, Spanish, and Catalan, based on a multilingual approach and aimed at teachers and students offers multimedia content and didactic sequences involving the use of audiovisual translation for the acquisition of plurilingual competence: http://citrans.uv.es/pluritav/sd/?lang=en

Language Learning with *Netflix*, a *Chrome* extension that allows viewers to watch films/programmes with two subtitles on at the same time, so that they can visually pair translations with dialogue: https://languagelearningwithnetflix.com/

Two excellent initiatives that run creative translation workshops in schools:

Translators in schools: http://translatorsinschools.org/

Shadow heroes: https://shadowheroes.org/

Action-oriented approaches
being at the heart of the action

Aline Germain-Rutherford[1]

Potential impact	medium
Timescale	ongoing
Keywords	action-oriented, scenarios, task-based, community-based

What is it?

An action-oriented approach views

> "users and learners of a language primarily as 'social agents', i.e. members of society who have tasks (not exclusively language-related) to accomplish in a given set of circumstances, in a specific environment and within a particular field of action. While acts of speech occur within language activities, these activities form part of a wider social context, which alone is able to give them their full meaning" (Council of Europe, 2001, p. 9).

As 'social agents', learners fully engage in meaningful real-life situations to which they learn to respond in a wholly cognitive and emotional manner, mobilizing their unique linguistic and sociocultural repertoires. Here, the notion of 'task' goes beyond the mere notion of a communicative activity to encompass the realization of projects or problems to be solved rooted in reality, socially, and culturally situated, through a set of targeted and concerted 'social' actions, 'not exclusively language-related', to achieve a clearly defined objective. Whether

---

1. University of Ottawa, Ottawa, Ontario, Canada; agermain@uottawa.ca

How to cite: Germain-Rutherford, A. (2021). Action-oriented approaches: being at the heart of the action. In T. Beaven & F. Rosell-Aguilar (Eds), *Innovative language pedagogy report* (pp. 91-96). Research-publishing.net. https://doi.org/10.14705/rpnet.2021.50.1241

within the community in a community-based approach, or in the classroom, itself perceived as a mini-society with a social dimension (Puren, 2009), learners engage and collaborate with peers and others as they mobilize and acquire prior and new skills, knowledge, values, and know-how to solve real-life problems. Communication is not the goal, it is the means, along with critical thinking, self-reflection, creativity, and adaptability, to achieve the task.

It is because the action-oriented approach takes us closer to the authenticity of language exchanges, grounded in the complexity of the sociocultural realities of learners, of the tasks to complete and of the different contextual environments, that it is both so inspiring and so contemporary. Indeed, in an era where social media are omnipresent and there is an overload of information, the issue is no longer that of communicating with others. Working with others and collaborating with others "is the condition for a true understanding of the other" (Puren, 2006, p. 38). The action-oriented approach is a reflection of this societal transformation.

Examples

The first example illustrates how a community-based program for English language learners integrates an action-oriented approach to actively engage late arriving immigrant and refugee high school students in the United States to learn a new language, explore a new culture, and develop a sense of belonging in their new community. The Linking Learning, Belonging and Community program funded by a National Leadership Grant of the Institute of Museum and Library Services, is an inter-institutional project offered in public libraries, generally identified as inclusive centers for learning and community connectedness.

The design of the curriculum activities is based on technology-based and action-oriented projects, to develop language competencies along with skills such as critical thinking, problem solving, collaboration, leadership, and adaptability. The student-led projects prompt students to explore their new cultural environment, ask questions to community members, and take risks in their learning while offering them opportunities for reflection and dialog. This approach incorporates the sociocultural values and perspectives of the students and their own ethnic/

cultural backgrounds and brings them awareness of their new environment and culture. The personal and psychological benefits of collective problem solving that this project offers especially help the students to expand their social networks, build social capital, and begin to fulfill the fundamental human need to belong. The community-based activities also include student-led facilitated issues forums in which parents and community members are invited to participate. This dialog helps youth appreciate the value of their parents' culturally traditional approaches and help parents understand that their children are trying to find solutions acceptable in both their worlds.

Example of a scenario: Navigating my neighborhood community

- Your group is tasked to report about an association/organization of your neighborhood community that offers services and social activities for youth and families, as well as opportunities to be more involved in the life of the community. You will present and discuss this report to your peers, families, and community members.

- Explore and select one community association/organization.

- Collect and organize information about it.

- Identify opportunities of community and civic engagement in this association/organization

- Create a multimedia report to discuss in a visually engaging way the information you have collected, synthesized, and organized.

The second example comes from the Canadian Research Council funded research project – LINguistic and Cultural DIversity Reinvente (LINCDIRE). Based on an action-oriented approach, LINCDIRE embraces plurilingualism at its core by recognizing and mobilizing the unique linguistic and cultural repertoires of students in the language classroom. The process of language

Chapter 14. Action-oriented approaches

learning is organized around scenarios that lead students to accomplish real-life tasks and produce significant artifacts (see a collection of scenarios developed by language teachers: https://lite.lincdireproject.org/all-scenarios/).

Benefits

As learners actively engage in solving real-life problems or in creating purposeful projects, they not only are involved in meaningful communication, they are exposed to cognitively challenging content while searching, assessing, and organizing resources and information to achieve the tasks. Processing this content requires complex and higher-order thinking, allowing for learners to engage in meaningful and authentic intellectual work. Manipulating, transforming, synthesizing, explaining, and interpreting meaningful information, enhance knowledge retention, and understanding, and offer better chances to result in greater student engagement and academic achievement (European Commission, 2018; Holm, 2011; Newmann & Wehlage, 1993; Zohar & Dori, 2003).

Furthermore, an action-oriented curriculum, culturally inclusive as it takes into consideration the sociocultural values and perspectives of the student and his/her community, is conducive to improved learning outcomes. It helps develop a positive sense of self for the learner, whose multicultural and plurilingual identity is valued and respected (Cummins, 2011; Cummins & Early, 2011).

Finally, more than language skills, by placing the learner at the heart of the action, the action-oriented approach creates an environment and a dynamic conducive to the development of lifelong learning skills such as critical and creative thinking, resilience, intercultural competence, and autonomy (Little, 2006).

Potential issues

As Piccardo and North (2019) point out, although since the publication of the definition of the action-oriented approach by the Council of Europe (2001) many language teachers have intuitively implemented this approach, current language education still relies largely on methodologies removed from meaningful social interaction. Professional development to operate this social and real-life oriented shift is essential, and a challenge. Designing relevant real-life scenarios with all the core components of an action-oriented approach, transforming the roles of learners into social agents and teachers into facilitators, and assessing learning are difficult challenges.

Looking to the future

> Multiple factors, including important research in the field of cognitive development and neuroscience, have accumulated evidence of the importance of developing global and intercultural competencies to thrive in our globalized world. New access to opportunities and learning experiences offered by the Internet and current technologies point to a promising future for action-oriented approaches.
>
> Social media and Web 2.0 technology have opened language classrooms to the world, enabling language teachers and learners from all over the globe to interact with others, work on collaborative and interdisciplinary projects, acquire new knowledge and a better understanding of other ways of seeing the world, and develop greater cognitive flexibility, better problem solving, higher thinking skills and creative thinking. iEARN-International Education and Resource Network, eTwinning, BabelWeb, or the project e-lang are excellent examples of platforms facilitating such collaborations.
>
> From 'learner' to 'user' and 'social agent', the language learner is at the heart of the action.

References

Council of Europe. (2001). *A common European framework of reference for languages: learning, teaching, assessment.* Cambridge University Press.

Cummins, J. (2011). Literacy engagement: fueling academic growth for English learners. *The Reading Teacher, 65*(2), 142-146. https://doi.org/10.1002/trtr.01022

Cummins, J., & Early, M. (2011). *Identity texts: the collaborative creation of power in multilingual schools*. Trentham.

European Commission. (2018). *Proposal for a council recommendation on a comprehensive approach to the learning and learning of languages*. European Commission.

Holm, M. (2011). Project-based instruction: a review of the literature on effectiveness in prekindergarten through 12th grade classrooms. *InSight: Rivier Academic Journal, 7*(2), 1-13. https://www2.rivier.edu/journal/ROAJ-Fall-2011/J575-Project-Based-Instruction-Holm.pdf

Little, D. (2006). *Learner autonomy: drawing together the threads of self-assessment, goal setting and reflection*. European Language Portfolio Teacher Training. http://archive.ecml.at/mtp2/Elp_tt/Results/DM_layout/00_10/06/06%20Supplementary%20text.pdf

Newmann, F., & Wehlage, G. (1993). Five standards of authentic instruction. *Educational Leadership, 50*(7), 8-12.

Piccardo, E., & North, B. (2019). *The action-oriented approach: a dynamic vision of language education*. Multilingual Matters.

Puren, C. (2006). De l'approche communicative à la perspective actionnelle. *Le Français dans le Monde, 347*, 37-40.

Puren, C. (2009). Variations sur le thème de l'agir social en didactique des langues-cultures étrangères. *Les Langues Moderne*, 1-31. https://www.aplv-languesmodernes.org/spip.php?article1888

Zohar, A., & Dori, Y. J. (2003). Higher order thinking skills and low-achieving students: are they mutually exclusive? *The Journal of the Learning Science, 12*(2), 145-181. https://doi.org/10.1207/s15327809jls1202_1

Resource

You can find some action-oriented scenarios by CEFR level by Lite, the LINCDIRE online portfolio here: https://lite.lincdireproject.org/all-scenarios/

Digital corpora
language teaching and learning in the age of big data

Matt Absalom[1]

Potential impact	medium
Timescale	ongoing
Keywords	digital corpora, corpus linguistics, data-driven learning, language in context

What is it?

Using corpora to teach languages is nothing new and, while the term corpus linguistics hails from the 1940s, most language learning before the 20th century adopted a corpus approach – using a series of texts in the language under study as a type of corpus on which to base acquisition. With the advent of widespread computing in the latter half of the 20th century, corpora began to be digitised, rendering interrogation of large amounts of data a much simpler and more appealing prospect. Today, languages in all forms (written, spoken, performed, formal, informal, etc.) are captured all the time through online and digital platforms, apps, etc. meaning that the wealth of language data literally at our fingertips is enormous. This has triggered the development of appropriate tools to explore these vast data sets.

For language teaching and learning the possibilities fall into two categories: using existing corpora or creating your own corpora. A good place to start exploring language corpora is *Sketch Engine* (https://www.sketchengine.eu/corpora-and-languages/). You can sign up for a free 30 day trial and access all functions, featured corpora for all languages, as well as the corpus building capacities.

---

1. University of Melbourne, Melbourne, Australia; mabsalom@unimelb.edu.au; https://orcid.org/0000-0003-3539-8832

How to cite: Absalom, M. (2021). Digital corpora: language teaching and learning in the age of big data. In T. Beaven & F. Rosell-Aguilar (Eds), *Innovative language pedagogy report* (pp. 97-101). Research-publishing.net. https://doi.org/10.14705/rpnet.2021.50.1242

Which leads to the second type of activity: creating corpora. Apart from Sketch Engine, another relatively accessible option is *#LancsBox* (http://corpora.lancs. ac.uk/lancsbox/) which allows you to either interact with existing corpora or create your own.

Why use corpora? Applying corpora in your teaching and learning can support activities which involve inductive learning: analysing language to work out how something works, particularly in context. Utilising digital corpora, either those already available or creating your own customised corpora, streamlines this process as you can instantaneously produce all instances of, say, a particular grammatical feature or see how a word is used. You can also apply this to text types or genres – for instance, what do newspaper articles do that is different to short stories or how do people make doctor's appointments over the phone compared to making a hair appointment? Many online language sites take a corpus approach such as *Reverso Context* (https://context.reverso.net/translation/).

Example

A constant stumbling block for learners of Italian is the choice of preposition. This often comes from the simplistic one-to-one translations presented in language textbooks, manuals, etc. In order to sensitise students to the importance of context in the correct selection of prepositions, I devised an exercise which used a small corpus created from the two literary texts that were under study at the time – I thought this would be useful pedagogically, since the students were already reading these texts and therefore would approach the task with less anxiety and more familiarity. I imported the texts into #LancsBox to create the corpus and then created lists of concordances (Figure 1) which showed the prepositions, *a*, *di*, and *da* in context. I gave students a table (Figure 2) to complete which helped guide their mining of the data. Essentially, they had to transpose the occurrences of the preposition from the original concordance lists of contexts from the texts in question into columns which showed the diverse functions of the prepositions: e.g. locative, genitive, introducing an infinitive, etc.

```
Concordance Hits  169
Hit       KWIC
1                            che cosa ti costa dargli un po'    di acqua vegetominerale... Andiamo, per un po' di
2            ' di acqua vegetominerale... Andiamo, per un po'   di acqua vegeto... (più che mai deciso puntandogli
3                       capire di che si stia parlando, pur     di allontanare la minaccia) No, no, io non
4                     due? È talmente pazzo che sarebbe capace  di andare a costituirsi... presto... Presto, ferma
5                      scusa, caro... chi è la signora? (fingendo  di cadere dalle nuvole) Chi? Sono una moglie...
6                               di fare il furbo e non cercare  di camuffare anche la voce che tanto non
7                          ; il primo a parlare è il padrone    di casa) C'era proprio bisogno di fare
8                      a tener mano alle balordate del padrone  di casa! Eh no, eh no! Mi dispiace,
9                           sotto il tiro della pistola del padrone  di casa, non può fare a meno di
10            .. (strappando la pistola dalle mani del padrone  di casa e puntandola verso il marito) Ah,
11                      e potuto divorziare? (chiedendo aiuto al padrone  di casa) Eh? potuto? (chiede aiuto alla Moglie
12                        io non lo sapevo... (rivolto al padrone  di casa) Com'è che sono bigamo osservante?! (
13              . (entrano le due donne seguite dal padrone     di casa. Sono piuttosto scalmanate) (rivolgendosi
14                     sacco della refurtiva. Ma riecco i padroni  di casa) È rientrato dalla finestra, il furbacchion
15                       mi illudevo: "Mia moglie non è capace  di certe azioni... è una donna all'antica,
16                              telefonare? E a chi? A me no   di certo... Lei crede che lo sia da
17                           fa vivo e che perciò nulla ha     di che temere, torna sui suoi passi. Vorrebbe
18                  che andrà a spifferare tutto! (senza capire di che si stia parlando, pur di allontanare
19                  spiegarle l'inghippo. L'inghippo? L'inghippo di che? Sì, insomma, che siete stati voi
20                  due ad ubriacarmi... per non farmi parlare... di che cosa poi, lo sapete soltanto voi.
21                         di una certa banda Martello. (col tono di chi ripete a memoria) Banda Martello, composta
22                      la moglie del signor Tornati? La moglie   di chi?... Ma non facciamo scherzi ...Giulia è
23                    tira fuori dalla tasca un enorme mazzo    di chiavi) (rivolgendosi al marito) Quante chiavi!
24         munale, che come vicesindaco aveva celebrato più      di cinquanta matrimoni, si spara per adulterio". Ch
25                        hai fatto rinascere il rimorso, il senso di colpa... Scusami, non volevo. (si rialza, mette
26                   dre... stavamo mangiando... quando... mi ricordo di colpo d'essermi dimenticate a casa le
27                   bambini... È vero ti stavo appunto dicendo  di come mi piacciono i bambini... Già.... ma
28                       è certo tuo marito... Ma sei matto,     di'? Come puoi pensare queste cose? Non mentire...
29                    moglie? È sempre stata una donna piena    di complessi, di pregiudizi piccolo-borghesi... Mi
30                  non abbia nemmeno un po' di sensibilità...  di comprensione, almeno nei miei riguardi? Non capi
31                           un cassetto e gli porge una manciata di cucchiai d'argento) Non vorrei approfittare dell
32                  I LADRI VENGONO PER NUOCERE ATTO UNICO      di DARIO FO PERSONAGGI LADRO MOGLIE DEL LADRO
33                    centro della stanza) ma a chi credi       di darla a bere? La telefonata, l'equivoco,
34             tanto il Ladro, piuttosto spaventato, ha cercato  di darsi alla fuga attraverso la finestra, ma
35                                  l'ho mai detto. È il tipo   di dirlo... avanti, prenda anche questi... (apre un
36                  'ora in poi, fai anche a meno              di dirmi dove vai perché tanto a me...
37                  evidentemente non riesce a trattenere gli ahi di dolore procuratigli dalla grossa pendola sbattut
38                      'altro capo del filo sento una voce    di donna che m'insulta Ero da mia
39                          che non è altro... ma non crederà    di dormire 293. LADRO 294. UOMO 295
40                    . Mi fa piacere, così avrà la fortuna    di essere seppellito in un suolo consacrato... Com
41                   256.  LADRO  UOMO LADRO   (cercando       di essere il più possibile naturale) Ah, sei
42                  ... (che comincia a innervosirsi. Fa il gesto di estrarre la pistola dalla tasca) Se proprio
```

Figure 1. Example of list of concordances of preposition di

Verbi che vogliono di quando seguiti da un infinito Per es.: ha finito di mangiare	Espressioni che vogliono di quando seguite da un infinito Per es.: sono capace di farlo	Espressioni idiomatiche con di Per es.: di buon'ora	Uso possessivo Per es.: il libro di lei	Altri usi Da definire

Figure 2. Example of table for students to complete: la preposizione di

Benefits

Existing language corpora provide endless examples of language in context in diverse registers, genres, time periods, and text dimensions. While predominantly text-based, there are also corpora of recorded language whether spontaneous, televised/broadcast, or scripted. Importantly, the work of constructing these language banks has already been done (and continues).

For those with developed Information Technology (IT) literacy, corpora tools offer a lot of scope for exploration of language and data-driven learning. Teachers can custom-build their own corpora or customise existing corpora. Students too can be instructed to use corpora tools to investigate how language works through accessing large arrays of exemplar texts.

Potential issues

The most glaring issue with digital corpora is technology. Corpus linguistics is the province of computer scientists and linguists and, while software tools are becoming more user friendly, building and interrogating corpora still require a significant effort even for those with reasonable IT skills.

In the example above, I decided to avoid wrestling with students' capacity to use the software to access the corpus and provide them with an excerpt myself. This was largely because the year before this I had asked the previous group of students to download software, read the manual, load the corpus, and then carry out various tasks which remained beyond the majority of my students. The focus of my class was not corpus linguistics, this was simply a different way to approach the study of Italian so, in some respects, it is too much to expect language students to (want to) learn how to use digital corpora. Additional issues relate to accessibility of digital corpora which might be problematic for students with learning or physical disabilities, or limited access to technology. Finally, not all languages have the same number or variety of corpora readily available online.

Looking to the future

> There is no doubt that we will continue to amass massive amounts of (language) data. It is also the case that digital corpora will lead to more nuanced development of translation and AI-supported language tools. Taking advantage of these developments and accessing digital corpora to support language learning, both in and outside formal settings, offers great potential for our students to experience languages in all their glory.

Resources

Boulton, A., & Landure, C. (2016). Using corpora in language teaching, learning and use. *Research and Teaching Languages for Specific Purposes, 35*(2). https://doi.org/10.4000/apliut.5433

Flowerdew, J. (2009). Corpora in language teaching. In M. H. Long and C. J. Doughty (Eds), *The handbook of language teaching* (pp. 327-350). Willey Blackwell. https://doi.org/10.1002/9781444315783.ch19

#LancsBox corpus toolbox: http://corpora.lancs.ac.uk/lancsbox/

Reverso Context contextual dictionary: https://context.reverso.net/translation/

Sketch Engine, a corpus manager and text analysis tool: https://www.sketchengine.eu/corpora-and-languages/

Digital storytelling
multimodal meaning making

Judith Buendgens-Kosten[1]

Potential impact	medium
Timescale	short term
Keywords	storytelling, multiliteracies, interactive fiction

What is it?

Robin (n.d.) defines digital storytelling as "the practice of using computer-based tools to tell stories", stressing that "they all revolve around the idea of combining the art of telling stories with a variety of multimedia, including graphics, audio, video, and Web publishing" (n.p.). Ohler (2009) suggests that

> "digital storytelling […] uses personal digital technology to combine a number of media into a coherent narrative" (p. 15).

Very often, digital storytelling involves some kind of video production (see examples on https://digitalstorytelling.coe.uh.edu).

Including stories and storytelling for language learning barely needs justification. The ability to tell a story is important in many life settings, from hanging out with friends to selling a product. But why *digital* storytelling? In 1996 The New London Group argued that the traditional perspective on literacy should be extended to encompass a broader range of meaning-making practices, including

---

1. Goethe University Frankfurt, Frankfurt, Germany; buendgens-kosten@em.uni-frankfurt.de; https://orcid.org/0000-0003-2852-8539

How to cite: Buendgens-Kosten, J. (2021). Digital storytelling: multimodal meaning making. In T. Beaven & F. Rosell-Aguilar (Eds), *Innovative language pedagogy report* (pp. 103-108). Research-publishing.net. https://doi.org/10.14705/rpnet.2021.50.1243

those involving digital media. In a similar vein, The Douglas Fir Group (2016) argues that "language learning is semiotic learning" (p. 27), and goes beyond the acquisition of words and structures.

While engaging in digital storytelling, learners practise the target language in a potentially highly motivating context, use the target language and other linguistic resources to engage in discussion and negotiation about the process, and in the production of their stories (e.g. in a task-based language teaching tradition); also extending their repertoire of meaning-making resources through practice and reflection – cf. The New London Group's (1996) notion of critical framing. Students of many different levels of proficiency can create engaging digital stories – from the A1-level primary school student telling a story via the Puppet Pals app, to the adult language learner engaging in a complex cross-media storytelling project.

Examples

Creating interactive fiction:

> Your teacher caught you cheating on your vocabulary test. They confront you. Do you:
>
> - [[deny any wrongdoing]]
> - [[admit to cheating]]
> - [[try to change topics]]

Interactive fiction refers to branching stories in which narrative sections and/or dialogues are interspersed with decisions the player/reader makes, which impact how the story continues.

When creating interactive fiction, students can draw on experiences with a broad range of interactive fiction types, from interactive films such as Bandersnatch, to popular games and apps such as '80 Days', or even traditional, 1980s-style

'Choose your own adventure' books (which are available in language learner-friendly formats, from A1 level onwards, e.g. in the Oxford Bookworms and Helwig series of graded readers). Many computer games can also serve as inspiration.

Branching stories can become very complex very fast. Using authoring software such as Twine (twinery.org, see also Ford, 2016), can help keep an increasingly-entangled web of story nodes under control. But of course knowing how to use authoring software is only one step towards creating a great piece of interactive fiction. The FanTALES project (https://www.fantales.eu/results/) has published a card-based interactive storytelling tutorial that combines a step-by-step approach in learning to use Twine with instruction and inspiration regarding the craft of storytelling, using popular contemporary stories as a backdrop.

A single telegram text can be the beginning of a love story, or the first step down a slippery slope. A harmless enough WhatsApp conversation can turn from funny to scary and back to funny in just a few typed words, a single audio message, and some emoji or photos.

With the search term 'texting story', or the combination of a chat app brand name and 'fake' or 'simulator', you will find many different commercial apps that help with the creation of stories in the shape of fake chats.

Taking The Douglas Fir Group's (2016) assertion to heart that "language learning is identity work" (p. 31), such chat simulators provide rich opportunities to let learners draw on semiotic resources and identity aspects that are rarely in the forefront in the foreign language classroom, e.g. informal registers, translanguaging skills, (partially) conventionalised use of visual resources such as emoji and memes, as well as combinations of written and spoken language. With their dialogue structure and the opportunity to draw on a wide range of semiotic resources, chat simulators can enable beginners to tell a coherent story, while also providing advanced language learners with interesting design options.

Chapter 16. Digital storytelling

Benefits

The ability to 'tell a story' is not only of relevance in the creative professions. Teachers, salespeople, journalists, and political activists all depend on communicating their knowledge and ideas in memorable ways. Digital storytelling is an established element of advertising and public relations.

Digital storytelling provides students with the opportunity to develop – and to showcase – their multimodal meaning-making skills, to play with languages and genres, to be creative, and to inspire others. Furthermore, from a language learning perspective, digital storytelling has a lot of potential as it can provide opportunities to focus on planning and revision of texts, as well as for negotiation of meaning if done collaboratively. When products are to be published, aspects of linguistic accuracy and social appropriacy, as well of audience design, may play a role too.

Potential issues

Some tools for digital storytelling are very powerful – and complex. Authoring tools that may have fewer settings, but require little to no instruction, might be a better fit in contexts in which only little time is available for a digital storytelling mini-project.

Also, care should be taken that the tools chosen are fully accessible for language learners. Some authoring tools may not be suitable for students with visual impairments or difficulties with fine motor control, for example. Fortunately, the market for authoring tools (commercial and non-commercial alike) is large, providing many different options.

While most learners will have some experience with non-linear storytelling and chat-based communication, providing learners with sample stories can be helpful for those with less experience or few ideas about how to translate their experience into a new story.

Looking to the future

> Digital storytelling will develop in parallel with changes in our media environment. Virtual reality digital storytelling is already used in some schools. On one hand, as prices drop and hardware becomes more widely available, virtual reality storytelling will likely be adopted more broadly. On the other hand, as some media and genres lose popularity, their role for digital storytelling will also wane (e.g. blog-based digital storytelling).
>
> When The New London Group (1996) discussed the need for a new understanding of literacy, they also stressed the need for learners to be able to engage in plurilingual meaning making, including "the code-switching often to be found within a text among different languages, dialects, or registers" (p. 69). Digital storytelling that includes plurilingual practices, or that is designed to appeal to users with different sets of linguistic resources, may play an increasing role in the future.

References

Ford, M. (2016). *Writing interactive fiction with Twine: play inside a story*. QUE.

Ohler, J. (2009). *Digital storytelling in the classroom. New media pathways to literacy, learning, and creativity*. Corwin Press. https://doi.org/10.4135/9781452277479

Robin, B. (n.d.). *What is digital storytelling?* Educational uses of digital storytelling. https://digitalstorytelling.coe.uh.edu/page.cfm?id=27&cid=27&sublinkid=29

The Douglas Fir Group (2016). A transdisciplinary framework for SLA in a multilingual world. *The Modern Language Journal, 100*(S1), 19-47. https://doi.org/10.1111/modl.12301

The New London Group. (1996). A pedagogy of multiliteracies: designing social futures. *Harvard Educational Review, Spring*, 60-93. https://doi.org/10.17763/haer.66.1.17370n67v22j160u

Chapter 16. Digital storytelling

Resources

Educational uses of digital storytelling can be found here: https://digitalstorytelling.coe.uh.edu

FanTALES Interactive Storytelling Tutorials: https://www.fantales.eu/results/

A short course (MOOC) on Powerful tools for teaching and learning: digital storytelling: https://www.coursera.org/learn/digital-storytelling

Twine, an open-source tool for telling interactive, nonlinear stories: www.twinery.org

Gamification
motivating language learning with gameful elements

Joan-Tomàs Pujolà[1]

Potential impact	high
Timescale	ongoing
Keywords	gamification, gamefulness, engagement, motivation, rewards

What is it?

Gamification is a methodological strategy that uses "game design elements in non-game contexts" (Deterding, Dixon, Khaled, & Nacke, 2011, p. 10). The purpose of gamification is to engage people, motivate action, promote learning, and solve problems (Kapp, 2012). There are other educational approaches that use playful components but are different from gamification, such as game-based learning or serious games. In those two cases, all kinds of games (digital video games, table games, outdoor games, etc.) or educational games are used to achieve a learning goal. Within the language learning area, Reinhardt (2019) opts for the global concept of 'gamefulness' which embraces all types of vernacular games, serious games, and gamification.

Different taxonomies of the game elements have been classified for gamification purposes. Among these classifications, Werbach and Hunter (2012) present the game elements in a hierarchy, the Dynamics, Mechanics, and Components (DMC) Pyramid, identifying three categories: dynamics, aspects such as *constraints*, *progression*, or *narrative*; mechanics, basic processes that drive the action forward such as *challenge*, *competition*, or *rewards*; and components,

---

1. Universitat de Barcelona, Barcelona, Spain; jtpujola@ub.edu; https://orcid.org/0000-0002-8664-432X

How to cite: Pujolà, J.-T. (2021). Gamification: motivating language learning with gameful elements. In T. Beaven & F. Rosell-Aguilar (Eds), *Innovative language pedagogy report* (pp. 109-114). Research-publishing.net. https://doi.org/10.14705/rpnet.2021.50.1244

the specific instantiations of mechanics and dynamics such as *avatars*, *badges*, *leaderboards*, *levels*, or *points*.

As mentioned in Pujolà and Appel (2020), Kapp (2012) distinguishes two types of gamification: structural and content. Structural gamification refers to a model in which the structure of the learning tasks is gamified without modifying the content. The main aim of this type of gamification is to engage students through rewards using, for instance, Points, Badges, and Leaderboards (PBL). Content gamification, on the other hand, implies changing the learning content to make it more like a game or video game, such as including a narrative in which challenges related to the story must be solved to achieve the objectives of the course.

Examples

The following examples are Spanish content gamifications that integrate different game elements and use a variety of technologies:

- Acedo's (2019) *La liga de la justicia y los superhéroes españoles* (Justice league and Spanish superheroes); and

- Niño's (2020) *Ciudad de todos* (City for all).

These projects have the following relevant features in common:

- they integrate and intertwine various game elements to make sure that different types of learners interact positively with them;

- PBL are not the only game elements introduced so their gamification interventions go beyond the most common reward mechanism;

- the narrative in each case helps to integrate the game elements, the learning tasks, and the use of technologies in a coherent way;

- the goals to be achieved in the gamified tasks are moderately challenging with increased complexity and clear progress; and

- feedback and rewards are provided within a short time.

Benefits

Gamification can be used in all educational contexts from primary to adult education and can be applied in any pedagogical approach: communicative, flipped classroom, or task-based learning. Gamified educational environments should create learning conditions to increase students' engagement, to activate their learning, to develop their autonomy, and thus, to motivate them.

The development of motivation in gamification starts with the students' involvement with the gamification processes, with their desire to take an active part in them. In that sense, choice is a relevant component by which students learn how to take decisions for successful learning and also constant feedback, as happens in video games, is indispensable for students to advance in the gamified learning context. A well-planned gamified instructional design allows for the development of multiple learning strategies and language learning competences.

Research to date has mostly focused on student engagement, motivation, or affective factors with mixed results (Homer, Hew, & Tan, 2018; Sailer, Hense, Mayr, & Mandl, 2017). As for language performance, most studies report some positive outcomes mainly on vocabulary learning according to Dehghanzadeh et al. (2019) or others on the development of pronunciation (Barcomb & Cardoso, 2020).

How can it be implemented?

Gamification can be implemented with or without technology. Nevertheless, the use of technology helps teachers keep record of the whole process in a gamified context and makes the teaching and learning processes more accessible. There is a diverse variety of platforms, apps, and tools for teachers to use when implementing gamification in their teaching. Four approaches to use different Information and Communication Technologies (ICTs) when gamifying can be established according to Pujolà and Appel (2020):

- gamification platforms that help to set up and manage gamified lessons or entire courses: Classcraft, ClassDojo, or Gradecraft;

- gamified quizzes that help teachers improve lesson interaction and also build gamified tests for assessment purposes: Kahoot!, Socrative, or Quizalize;

- game-like features and plugins introduced in regular virtual learning environments such as Moodle: e.g. Quizventure, Level Up!, or Ranking Block; and

- different ICTs used when implementing a gamified teaching intervention: Voki, Makebadges, Genially, or Pointagram.

There are also other learning platforms like Duolingo, Drops, or Memrise, mainly for self-learning with a rather traditional rote learning approach, that use gamification elements such as points, levels, or trophies to encourage users to continue progressing through the contents of the course practising mainly vocabulary, grammar, pronunciation, and translation (for further information on these platforms, see Jueru, Ferrão, Vitória, & Ferrão Silva, 2020).

Looking to the future

> Gamification is a pedagogical trend with great potential and a positive effect on student engagement but it is still to be proved that the increase of motivation results in better learning outcomes (Dehghanzadeh et al., 2019). However, the constant increase of gamification teaching experiences in language education should

help to carry out more research studies dealing with issues such as learning gains in different language areas. More empirical and systematic studies should focus on the development of language skills and language learning strategies that confirm gamification as an effective methodological strategy.

References

Acedo, J. R. (2019). *La liga de la justicia y los superhéroes españoles* (Justice league and Spanish superheroes). https://juanrafaelacedo.wixsite.com/ligajusticia

Barcomb, M., & Cardoso, W. (2020). Rock or lock? Gamifying an online course management system for pronunciation instruction: focus on English /r/ and /l/. *CALICO Journal, 37*(2), 127-147. https://doi.org/10.1558/cj.36996

Dehghanzadeh, H., Fardanesh, H., Hatami, J., Talaee, E., & Noroozi, O. (2019). Using gamification to support learning English as a second language: a systematic review. *Computer Assisted Language Learning*. https://doi.org/10.1080/09588221.2019.1648298

Deterding, S., Dixon, D., Khaled, R., & Nacke, L. (2011). From game design elements to gamefulness. *Proceedings of the 15th International Academic MindTrek Conference on Envisioning Future Media Environments - MindTrek '11* (pp. 9-15). https://doi.org/10.1145/2181037.2181040

Homer, R., Hew, K., & Tan, C. (2018). Comparing digital badges-and-points with classroom token systems: effects on elementary school ESL students' classroom behavior and English learning. *Journal of Educational Technology & Society, 21*(1), 137-151. http://www.jstor.org/stable/26273875

Jueru, T., Ferrão, S., Vitória, F., Ferrão Silva, R. (2020). Gamification for technology-enhanced language learning (TELL) – success factors of gamified language learning platform design. *Revista Iberoamericana de Informática Educativa, 31*, 54-69. http://iecom.adie.es/index.php/IECom/article/view/334

Kapp, K. M. (2012). *The gamification of learning and instruction: case-based methods and strategies for training and education.* Pfieffer: An Imprint of John Wiley & Sons.

Niño, J. (2020). *Ciudad de todos* (City for all). https://sites.google.com/view/ciudad-de-todos/inicio

Pujolà, J. T., & Appel, C. (2020). Gamification for technology-enhanced language teaching and learning. In M. Kruk & M. Peterson (Eds), New technological applications for foreign and second language learning and teaching (ch. 5). IGI Global. https://doi.org/10.4018/978-1-7998-2591-3.ch005

Reinhardt, J. (2019). Gameful second and foreign language teaching and learning. Palgrave-Macmillan. https://doi.org/10.1007/978-3-030-04729-0

Sailer, M., Hense, J. U., Mayr, S. K., & Mandl, H. (2017). How gamification motivates: an experimental study of the effects of specific game design elements on psychological need satisfaction. *Computers in Human Behavior*, *69*, 371-380. https://doi.org/10.1016/j.chb.2016.12.033

Werbach, K., & Hunter, D. (2012). *For the win: how game thinking can revolutionize your business*. Wharton Digital Press.

Resource

Practical guide to gamification in Spanish: Acedo, J. R. (2019). *Guía práctica para una gamificación en ELE*. https://es.scribd.com/document/435018588/Hip

Augmented reality learning
education in real-world contexts

Mark Pegrum[1]

Potential impact	high
Timescale	long term
Keywords	augmented reality, real-world contexts, immersive technology, embodied learning, situated learning

What is it?

Augmented Reality (AR) bridges the real and the digital. It is part of the Extended Reality (XR) spectrum of immersive technological interfaces. At one end of the continuum, Virtual Reality (VR) immerses users in fully digital simulations which effectively substitute for the real world. At the other end of the continuum, AR allows users to remain immersed in the real world while superimposing digital overlays on the world. The term *mixed reality*, meanwhile, is sometimes used as an alternative to AR and sometimes as an alternative to XR.

In a broad conceptual view, AR refers to the dynamic presentation, in a real-world setting, of digital information and communication channels which are contextually relevant (with certain non-contextualised exceptions such as some app-based 3D models); in a narrower technocentric view, AR refers to the "direct superimposition of digital information and communication channels on our perceptions of a real-world setting" (Pegrum, 2019, p. 57). While XR headsets allow for truly immersive experiences, AR is currently most commonly seen on smartphones (or tablets) where AR browsers or apps overlay digital text, images, videos, and/or 3D objects, which may or may not

---

1. The University of Western Australia, Perth, Australia; mark.pegrum@uwa.edu.au; https://orcid.org/0000-0003-1577-4642

How to cite: Pegrum, M. (2021). Augmented reality learning: education in real-world contexts. In T. Beaven & F. Rosell-Aguilar (Eds), *Innovative language pedagogy report* (pp. 115-120). Research-publishing.net. https://doi.org/10.14705/rpnet.2021.50.1245

be interactive, on a user's view of the real-world environment as registered through the phone's camera and displayed on its screen (see Figure 1). AR overlays may be triggered by visual markers (at the simplest, QR codes), AI-powered object recognition, and/or location (generally using GPS or Bluetooth). As AR is advancing, the conceptual and technocentric definitions are in the process of merging, with the direct superimposition of digital data on our perceptions becoming the norm.

Figure 1. Times Square, New York City, seen through the Wikitude AR browser. Source: Wikitude, under CC BY-SA 2.0 licence, from www.flickr.com/photos/wikitude/30944213892/

Pedagogically, AR invites three main uses (MacCallum & Parsons, 2019). It can be used for *information transmission* activities where students access learning materials, authored by their teachers or external experts, in context; for *(social) constructivist* activities where students individually or collaboratively record, annotate, interact with, and/or modify elements of their virtual or real settings; and for *constructionist* activities where students employ today's user-friendly tools to design and build AR artefacts or experiences, potentially even making this user-generated content available to support others' learning.

Examples

Inside the classroom, language teachers have enhanced learning materials through the use of AR tools like *ARientation, Augment,* and *Aurasma/HP Reveal* (the last of these now discontinued). These enable students to scan textbooks, handouts, or cards with a smartphone to reveal images, videos, polls, or discussion boards. But the possibilities are far greater outside the classroom, where language teachers have used AR tools like *ARIS* (Field Day), *FreshAiR* (MoGo Mobile), *Pocket Trips* (LDR), and *Trail Shuttle* (Rockmoon) to build learning trails which are akin to gamified scavenger hunts. Accessed by students on phones or tablets, they typically consist of a series of real-world stations where students receive a digital question to answer or problem to solve and, in so doing, are led to the next station on the trail.

Figure 2. Girls interacting with an AR overlay on an LDR LocoMole trail in Chinatown, Singapore; reproduced with kind permissions from © LDR

In the *Explorez!* mobile game in Canada (2014-present, built with ARIS), the English-speaking campus of the University of Victoria, British Columbia, is overlaid with a virtual French campus. Students act as personal assistants to an imagined Francophone celebrity visitor, practising their spoken French as they carry out tasks in various campus locations and make recommendations to

Chapter 18. Augmented reality learning

enhance the celebrity's visit. In the *Surviving Alaska* mobile game in the USA (2014-present, also built with ARIS), primary school children who have been learning bilingually in English and Yup'ik (an Alaskan Native language) play the role of survivors of an apocalypse. After watching elders explain traditional knowledge in Yup'ik-language videos geotagged to relevant locations around the local village, they seek additional information through interviews with other elders and then demonstrate their learning by, for example, building a shelter or finding medicinal plants. In the *Fukuchiyama Castle Rally* in Japan (2017, built with Blippar), new undergraduate students from the University of Fukuchiyama worked in teams to locate AR cards containing contextually relevant English vocabulary, collecting secret codes along the way which allowed them to open a locked box at the end of their mission. On the *Torrens Walkabout Trail* in Australia (2018-present, built with My Tours), students taking English classes at the University of South Australia get to know Adelaide with the support of situated multimedia materials, record their own multimodal responses to their environment, practise relevant language, and ultimately develop their descriptive writing.

On the *Interactive Heritage Trails* in Singapore (2008-present, built with Pocket Trips), which have a social studies focus but incorporate elements of language and literacy, school students explore their city station by station. In a three-step process, students' handheld devices present multimedia materials to deepen their contextual understandings, pose factual questions they can answer using locally available information, and finally invite their collaborative, multimodal responses to their real-world learning environment, typically in the form of videos to be shared later with their teacher and classmates (for an example of a newer trail by the same company, see Figure 2). Meanwhile, students have successfully worked with authoring software such as Pocket Trips and Trail Shuttle to construct stations on learning trails, or indeed entire learning trails, for their peers, honing their own language skills in the process.

Benefits

Because AR, unlike VR, works with, rather than against, our embodiment and embeddedness in everyday real-world contexts, it supports learning that is embodied and active; situated, contextualised, and place-based; and authentic and often informal. Furthermore, because it bridges the real and the digital, and facilitates a continuation of learning outside the usual places and times of education, AR supports seamless learning across contexts (even if specific learning experiences may be contextualised). Using, and especially developing, AR content fosters a range of digital literacies, including multimodal, spatial, information, and coding literacy.

The emerging empirical research literature has found AR to be motivating for students, especially when fused with gaming elements. It seems increasingly clear that AR offers benefits for certain content – for example, concrete descriptive language (Pegrum, 2019) – and certain learners, but more research is needed to definitively establish exactly when and where it is of greatest value for language learning.

Potential issues

Current technological issues include the limited screen size and field of view on phones (Sailer, Rudi, Kurzhals, & Raubal, 2019), the cost of immersive headsets (though this is falling), the data demands (though 5G will help), and the lack of interoperability of software (though this will likely come with time). Educational issues, beyond the accessibility of hardware, software, and internet connectivity, include the need to move past using AR for its own sake and to identify its specific benefits. Issues with cognitive overload and distraction, and with privacy and surveillance, may be addressed in part through the development of attentional literacy and personal/security literacy, respectively.

Looking to the future

> As we move from smartphones to headsets, smart glasses, and even smart contact lenses, and as input mechanisms come to routinely include voice, gesture, and eye tracking, AR will offer an ever more immersive and seemingly natural experience. Importantly, as

> our technology increasingly facilitates the transmission of spatial audio and haptics, and very likely eventually smell and taste, AR will also offer a more multisensory experience. In education, this will mean access to more varied learning materials, more modes of collaboration, and more possibilities for self-expression.

References

MacCallum, K., & Parsons, D. (2019). Teacher perspectives on mobile augmented reality: the potential of Metaverse for learning. In *Proceedings of World Conference on Mobile and Contextual Learning 2019* (pp. 21-28). IAmLearn. https://www.learntechlib.org/p/210597/

Pegrum, M. (2019). *Mobile lenses on learning: languages and literacies on the move.* Springer. https://doi.org/10.1007/978-981-15-1240-7

Sailer, C., Rudi, D., Kurzhals, K., & Raubal, M. (2019). Towards seamless mobile learning with mixed reality on head-mounted displays. In *Proceedings of World Conference on Mobile and Contextual Learning 2019* (pp. 69-76). IAmLearn. https://www.learntechlib.org/p/210603/

Resources

Brown, M., McCormack, M., Reeves, J., Brooks, D. C., & Grajek, S. [with B. Alexander et al.]. (2020). *2020 EDUCAUSE Horizon Report: Teaching and Learning Edition.* EDUCAUSE. https://library.educause.edu/-/media/files/library/2020/3/2020_horizon_report_pdf.pdf

Papagiannis, H. (2017). *Augmented human: how technology is shaping the new reality.* O'Reilly Media.

Pegrum, M. (2019). Mobile AR trails and games for authentic language learning. In Y. Zhang & D. Cristol (Eds), *Handbook of mobile teaching and learning* (2nd ed.). Springer. https://doi.org/10.1007/978-981-13-2766-7_89

Pomerantz, J. (2020). Extending XR across campus: Year 2 of the EDUCAUSE/HP Campus of the Future Project. *EDUCAUSE.* https://www.educause.edu/ecar/research-publications/extending-xr-across-campus-year-2-of-the-educause-hp-campus-of-the-future-project/executive-summary-key-findings-acknowledgments

Traxler, J., & Kukulska-Hulme, A. (2016). (Eds). *Mobile learning: the next generation.* Routledge.

Automatic speech recognition
can you understand me?

Susana Pérez Castillejo[1]

Potential impact	medium
Timescale	medium term
Keywords	automatic speech recognition, pronunciation training, speech to print, feedback

What is it?

Automatic Speech Recognition (ASR) is a digital communication method that transforms spoken discourse into written text. This rapidly evolving technology is used in email, text messaging, or live video captioning. Current ASR systems operate in conjunction with Natural Language Processing (NLP) technology to transform speech into text that people – and machines – can read. NLP refers to the methodologies and computational tools that analyze data produced in a natural language, such as English.

When users talk into an ASR-enabled application, the speech signal turns into an audio file that is first filtered for background noise and then parsed into phonemes, which are the smallest sound units in a language: the word 'push', for example, has three phonemes ('p', 'u', and 'sh'). Through statistical probability, the ASR system analyzes the phoneme sequences it 'recognizes' and deduces the words that best match those sound strings. The auto-generated text can then be 'read' by a machine to perform some other tasks.

---

1. University of St. Thomas, Saint Paul, Minnesota, United States; pere9775@stthomas.edu; https://orcid.org/0000-0001-7543-4506

How to cite: Pérez Castillejo, S. (2021). Automatic speech recognition: can you understand me? In T. Beaven & F. Rosell-Aguilar (Eds), *Innovative language pedagogy report* (pp. 121-126). Research-publishing.net. https://doi.org/10.14705/rpnet.2021.50.1246

Self-study is the most frequent pedagogical approach taken when integrating ASR into language education, as it usually mediates learner-device interactions instead of learner-learner exchanges.

ASR is effectively used for pronunciation training (Pennington & Rogerson-Revell, 2019), but more recent uses (Istrate, 2019; Liakin, Cardoso, & Liakina, 2015; Nickolai, 2015) show that ASR can also promote oral skills beyond pronunciation.

Examples

iSpraak.com (Nickolai, 2015), a cloud-based ASR tool, 'listens' to how a student pronounces a text provided by the teacher and returns a similarity score based on native speech patterns. The auto-scoring feature encourages independent study: learners keep practicing until they reach a certain score, but the teacher does not need to listen to every file produced.

Auto-generated transcripts from speech-to-text engines such as *Microsoft Stream* can also support independent language development (Liakin et al., 2015). As learners compare what the tool 'understood' to what they were trying to say, they improve their performance. Some of these tools pair ASR with automated translation, which can further help learners self-assess their accuracy.

An emerging ASR application is the use of Virtual Assistants (VA) such as *Alexa* or *Siri* (Istrate, 2019; see also Underwood, this volume). The communicative functions that VAs motivate include uttering commands ("Alexa, play some music!") or asking factual questions ("Siri, what is the weather like in Tokyo today?"). Successfully getting a VA to perform the desired action or to provide the needed information requires not only pronunciation accuracy, but also some knowledge of L2 vocabulary and sentence structure: the learners are not reading or repeating model sentences. If the task involves asking questions and using the information obtained, listening comprehension is an additional skill practiced.

Benefits

Using ASR for pronunciation training may encourage learner autonomy: the immediate feedback provided by the software, in the form of a transcript or an accuracy score, makes learners more aware of their progress, and the ability to carry out the exercises without the teacher gives them more control over their practice.

Speaking tasks with VAs also increase speaking opportunities beyond the classroom. VAs are not suitable for conversational practice, yet, but producing the short action-oriented or information-seeking utterances typical in these tasks is still a good proficiency-building exercise that can prepare learners for more involved oral discourses. In fact, frequent use of VAs for independent practice has been linked to significant improvements in L2 speaking proficiency (Dizon, 2020).

Potential issues

An important issue in ASR's pedagogical application is data privacy. As with other web-based interactions, exchanges with VAs produce personal data that could be commercially exploited. Thus, it is important for educators to be mindful of the data privacy policies for the technologies they use.

A second concern is robustness. ASR accuracy depends much on the acoustic conditions (performance suffers in noisy environments) and, most importantly for language educators, the speaker's experience with the language. Users often complain that the ASR tool 'detected the wrong thing', even though they know they were saying it right.

Although 'comprehension' of accented speech keeps improving, ASR performance is still not ideal when transcribing speech produced by low-proficiency learners. This issue may be resolved as more data from this type of learner becomes available. ASR accuracy with non-native speech has improved due to increased computing power and data availability from commercial sources

Chapter 19. Automatic speech recognition

(telephone-based transactions, for example). These sources of data, however, do not include low-proficiency speakers: who dares to complete a phone transaction in a language they are not fluent in?

EdTech companies offering data-based learning solutions hold the key to improve ASR's robustness: tools such as *Extempore* are using a wide range of non-native deidentified speech data in their servers for research and development (Figure 1).

Auto-generated transcripts that are still highly accurate with novice learners will be a welcome grading aid for teachers. Reading is faster than listening, particularly if the audio file is plagued with the long pauses typical in low-proficiency speech. While auto-generated fluency scores can indicate progress on the temporal aspects of speech (frequency and mean duration of pauses, percentage of speaking time), transcripts can help teachers provide feedback on lexical and syntactic accuracy faster.

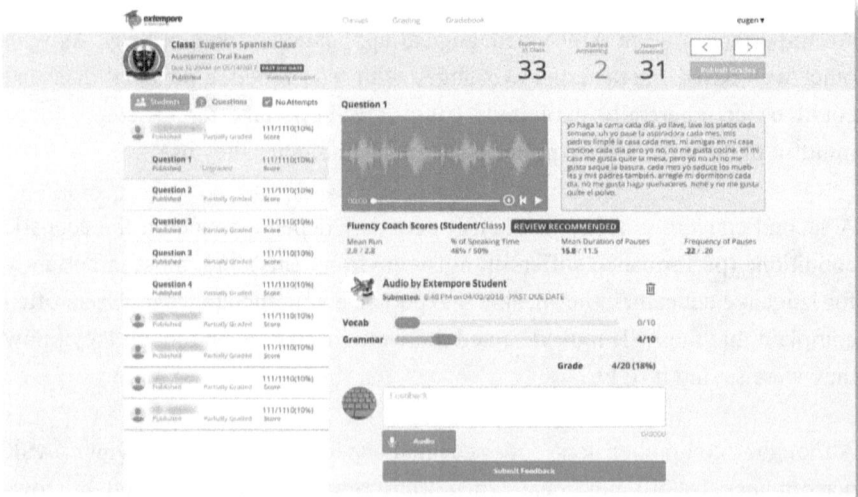

Figure 1. Prototype for Extempore's ASR-enhanced features. Metadata provided by ASR can assist language instructors when grading oral tasks

Looking to the future

> The pedagogical examples described above show that ASR technology can have an important impact in language teaching and learning: automated comparison with native speech patterns encourages pronunciation accuracy, self-access speaking tasks promote learner autonomy, and independent oral practice with VAs builds proficiency.
>
> There is a need for increased speaking practice outside the classroom targeting skills beyond pronunciation.
>
> Through robust ASR-enabled applications, this supplemental oral practice can be completed without necessarily turning into additional grading for the teacher. Thus, as ASR with low-proficiency speakers becomes more reliable, this technology will be more widely adopted for independent and classroom-based language learning.

References

Dizon, G. (2020). Evaluating intelligent personal assistants for L2 listening and speaking development. *Language Learning & Technology, 24*(1), 16-26. https://doi.org/10125/44705

Istrate, A. M. (2019). The impact of the virtual assistant (VA) on language classes. In *Proceedings of the 15th International Scientific Conference eLearning and Software for Education* (pp. 296-301). Carol I National Defense University.

Liakin, D., Cardoso, W., & Liakina, N. (2015). Learning L2 pronunciation with a mobile speech recognizer: French /y/. *Calico, 32*(1), 1-25. https://doi.org/10.1558/cj.v32i1.25962

Nickolai, D. (2015, October 30). iSpraak: automated online pronunciation feedback. *The FLTMAG.* http://www.fltmg.com

Pennington, M. C., & Rogerson-Revell, P. (2019). Using technology for pronunciation teaching, learning, and assessment. In *English Pronunciation Teaching and Research* (pp. 235-286). Palgrave Macmillan. https://doi.org/10.1057/978-1-137-47677-7_5

Underwood, J. (2021). Speaking to machines: motivating speaking through oral interaction with intelligent assistants. In T. Beaven & F. Rosell-Aguilar (Eds), *Innovative language pedagogy report* (pp. 127-132). Research-publishing.net. https://doi.org/10.14705/rpnet.2021.50.1247

Resource

For some advice on which ASR apps to try out, see: https://www.techradar.com/news/best-speech-to-text-app

Speaking to machines
motivating speaking through oral interaction with intelligent assistants

Joshua Underwood[1]

Potential impact	medium
Timescale	medium term
Keywords	automatic speech recognition, pronunciation training, practice, feedback

What is it?

Daring to voice new sounds, words, and phrases is an essential part of learning to speak a language. However, getting students, particularly in mono-lingual classes, to try to speak a foreign language can be a significant challenge. Voice interaction assistants, such as *Siri*, *Alexa*, or *Google Assistant*, offer new opportunities to create meaningful, fun tasks for language learning that require accurate spoken production. Designing good tasks requires an understanding of the learning context and needs as well as the interactional opportunities, constraints, and risks associated with any particular technology.

Recent studies suggest that instead of imagining home assistant voice interfaces as conversational, designers should think in terms of single turn request and response dialogues in which the response often serves as a resource that supports some other ongoing activity. For example, asking '*Alexa*, how do you spell awkward?' while writing an essay by hand, or checking a fact ('Hey *Google*, what's the population of London?') while arguing with another human. People mainly use voice interaction to get things done quickly and easily, to support

---

1. British Council, Bilbao, Spain; josh.underwood@gmail.com; https://orcid.org/0000-0002-1486-0429

How to cite: Underwood, J. (2021). Speaking to machines: motivating speaking through oral interaction with intelligent assistants. In T. Beaven & F. Rosell-Aguilar (Eds), *Innovative language pedagogy report* (pp. 127-132). Research-publishing.net. https://doi.org/10.14705/rpnet.2021.50.1247

Chapter 20. Speaking to machines

other activities, and for social fun. We explore pedagogic opportunities created by this kind of interaction; speaking **to** machines rather than speaking **with** machines (see Satar, this volume).

Example

Teachers quickly saw opportunities to use Intelligent Assistants (IA) as classroom assistants and to motivate speaking. Examples include: setting timers and playing background music for activities; as a resource to support daily routines – e.g. finding out about today's weather in a different part of the world; and asking for spellings, definitions, synonyms, or checking facts to support individual or group work.

Benefits

Students, particularly young learners, often find this kind of interaction motivating and want to try their hand at getting a machine to do something using their voice. What is more, IAs can potentially answer factual questions teachers may not know the answers to, thus supporting students' curiosity. They can also act as resources to support group work and student-to-student conversations – imagine a device per group, thus potentially freeing up teachers to monitor, listen, and help more.

One way that language teachers can exploit these opportunities for language development is by designing tasks that push students to produce vocabulary or language structures we want them to start to acquire. This might be in the form of written worksheets designed to scaffold groups doing IA assisted research, e.g. find out about and compare two countries with prompts such as, population, climate, typical foods, capital city, etc. Students need to help each other formulate and produce accurate enough questions to get the information they need. Failures can prompt students to reflect on the accuracy of their own and others' speech, self and peer-correct, try again, and ask teachers and one another for help. Such tasks give students a reason to produce and hear one another speaking the target language and may lead to them speaking it with one another.

Additional benefits of these kinds of activities are that efficient interaction with IAs requires students to listen carefully, as there is no visual feedback, and to think about and respect turn-taking, useful skills to work on in any language learning classroom.

Devices with screens and voice interaction offer different opportunities. For example, students might ask 'show me a picture of an artichoke' to support understanding while reading or listening. This not only helps students make multimodal associations but also gives feedback on their pronunciation as the device displays what it 'thinks' they said as text. This information can prompt learners to notice errors, self-correct, and/or ask for help. Teachers can also design tasks to help students notice typical sound difficulties e.g. 'show me a picture of a ship/sheep, cup/cap, lorry/lolly'.

Voice interaction can also be associated with physical changes, such as turning the lights off, thus creating multimodal and memorable associations. A long history of robot-assisted language learning suggests young learners may find speaking a foreign language to a robot much less intimidating than speaking to a human teacher or peer. Also, robots can move in response to speech and, particularly those that can recognise attention and simulate emotions, may encourage learners to make emotional associations with the language they use with possible benefits for meaningfulness and memory. Though this also raises ethical issues and opportunities to engage with these.

Potential issues

Many of the technologies mentioned are designed for individual use in a first language rather than for groups of language learners in educational settings. There are consequent issues and opportunities to resolve these.

Firstly, education systems need devices that comply with data protection regulations. Teachers also need materials that help them and their students discuss the risks and opportunities of voice interaction and agree on appropriate uses. This can lead to useful explorations of what any particular IA is capable of: Where are the opportunities and limitations? What questions can we ask to test our ideas? Learning to live with Artificial Intelligence (AI) and speak to machines seems likely to be an essential skill for the future.

Secondly, language learners and teachers need tailor-made Voice User Interfaces (VUIs). VUIs that not only support engaging tasks but also cope well with accents, typical classroom interactions (*What does... mean?*, *Could you explain...?*, *Could you say that again?*, etc.), multilingual input (e.g. *How do you say... in...?*), respond using language appropriate to a learner's competence level, and capture data useful for feedback on language. Teachers also need to reassess their roles in such an environment: how best can I use my time in this environment? What do I need to do to help students make the best use of these devices? For example, trying to and failing to communicate with an IA can quickly become frustrating. Teachers need to monitor, help overcome difficulties, and keep the atmosphere one of playful experimentation with new language.

Thirdly, with ethical automated data capture, opportunities to support teachers in assessment and in providing helpful feedback on speaking activities open up. Reversing the human request followed by device response model, one can imagine pairs of students in a class engaging in speaking tasks in response to device requests, e.g. *I'd like you to speak for two minutes about...*. It's very hard for a human teacher to monitor many simultaneous conversations in a classroom and students may well not feel they are being listened to and go off task. This situation might be improved by devices capturing what students say and providing transcripts, potentially with automated highlighting of possible errors and suggestions about opportunities to improve vocabulary range. Such information might be used by teachers and/or students to notice opportunities for improvements and provide motivating and helpful feedback.

To support this kind of human-machine collaboration, teachers and learners need to be involved in understanding the opportunities and risks, agreeing on acceptable uses, and designing desirable ways roles might be shared with 'cobot teachers'. This kind of conversation in turn can lead to a useful reassessment of what makes humans and human communication different to machines and what makes human teachers special.

Looking to the future

> Here we have focused on speaking to machines, rather than with machines, and on motivating speaking amongst groups of learners in classroom settings. This is about creating an atmosphere that encourages speaking in the target language and fosters human-to-human activity and conversation. Here technology does not replace teachers but rather acts as a helpful resource.
>
> This is a distinct opportunity to the more conversational and individualised uses of voice interaction in environments like Alelo's Enskill. Opportunities for conversation and freer-speaking practice with AIs are undoubtedly coming (see Google's recent Meena chatbot experiments), though interactions with these may too be exploited for classroom and group learning and help us to focus on and identify what is special and different about speaking with a human.

Reference

Satar, M. (2021). Speaking with machines: interacting with bots for language teaching and learning. In T. Beaven & F. Rosell-Aguilar (Eds), *Innovative language pedagogy report* (pp. 133-138). Research-publishing.net. https://doi.org/10.14705/rpnet.2021.50.1248

Resources

Carrier, M. (2017). Automated speech recognition in language learning: potential models, benefits and impact. *Training Language and Culture, 1*(1), 48-65. http://doi.org/10.29366/2017tlc.1.1.3

Tai, T. Y., & Chen, H. H. J. (2020). The impact of Google Assistant on adolescent EFL learners' willingness to communicate. *Interactive Learning Environments*, 1-18. https://doi.org/10.1080/10494820.2020.1841801

Van den Berghe, R., Verhagen, J., Oudgenoeg-Paz, O., van der Ven, S., & Leseman, P. (2019). Social robots for language learning: a review. *Review of Educational Research, 89*(2), 259-295. https://doi.org/10.3102%2F0034654318821286

Google Home in the classroom – the perfect teacher assistant https://www.bookwidgets.com/blog/2018/01/google-home-in-the-classroom-the-perfect-teacher-assistant

Interactive: try out Cambridge English write & improve or the speak & improve beta: https://speakandimprove.com/

Interactive: use your voice to get the dog to do something: https://www.dumplingthepug.com/pug-vr

News report about Finnish students learning a language from robots using the Elias app: https://youtu.be/O1qTVtFUxjw and https://www.softbankrobotics.com/

What schools need to know about voice assistants: https://edtechmagazine.com/k12/article/2020/09/what-schools-need-know-about-voice-assistants

Speaking with machines
interacting with bots for language teaching and learning

Müge Satar[1]

Potential impact	high
Timescale	long term
Keywords	chatbots, conversation, practice, specific tasks, interaction

What is it?

This piece explores technologies for freer communication *with* machines, i.e. bots (chatbots or conversational agents), rather than the concept of speaking *to* machines, such as Intelligent Assistants (IA) like *Alexa*. Bots are computer programmes which simulate natural intelligent communication using text or speech technologies. The first chatbot claimed to pass the Turing Test (a test to identify whether a computer is intelligent), ELIZA, was created by Joseph Weizenbaum in 1966 to imitate a psychotherapist. More recently, interest in chatbots appears to have shifted from whether they can be perceived as human to their ability to imitate natural conversations to achieve specific purposes and provide efficient customer services.

The field of Intelligent Computer Assisted Language Learning (ICALL) bridges research and practice in Artificial Intelligence (AI) and language learning (see Shultz & Heift, 2013). Language learners have been able to interact with many dialogue systems using short utterances since the 1990s. Modern chatbots use computational processes, such as Natural Language Processing and Machine

---

1. Newcastle University, Newcastle upon Tyne, United Kingdom; muge.satar@ncl.ac.uk; https://orcid.org/0000-0002-2382-6740

How to cite: Satar, M. (2021). Speaking with machines: interacting with bots for language teaching and learning. In T. Beaven & F. Rosell-Aguilar (Eds), *Innovative language pedagogy report* (pp. 133-138). Research-publishing.net. https://doi.org/10.14705/rpnet.2021.50.1248

Learning. An example of modern chatbots utilised for language learning was the introduction of bots in Duolingo, a popular language learning mobile phone application. Bots were only made available for the iOS operating system in October 2016 and were temporarily discontinued in April 2018. While bots have not yet come back, a quick search on the Duolingo app forum indicates their popularity (http://forum.duolingo.com/). User comments about the Duolingo bots particularly focus on availability of non-threatening conversational practice, opportunities to improve grammar, and immediate availability of bots as conversation partners. For instance, one forum user says:

> "I loved the feature of bots because it enables you to have a conversation without the stress of making mistakes, since you are not talking to a real person"

Example

A simple use of conversational agents in language learning would be to identify one or two chatbots, give learners a couple of conversation starters and example questions, and ask them to engage in a short conversation with the bots (see Yin & Satar, 2020). As an awareness-raising post-task activity, learners can reflect on their chat records to both focus on their language use and identify similarities and differences between chatbot and human interactions. A similar activity can be employed in language teacher training followed by a set of reflection questions to raise awareness on the limitations and affordances of chatbots, as follows.

- How easy/difficult was it for you to sustain the conversation with the chatbot?

- How coherent was the conversation?

- Did the chatbot acknowledge that it is a bot, or did it pretend to be human?

- What kind of questions or topics are bots better at answering?

- Are there any potentials for language learning in this activity (in terms of grammar, vocabulary, language skills, pragmatics: e.g. leave-takings, small talk, humour, negotiation for meaning, etc.)?

Benefits

There are many benefits to communicating with computers for language learners. First, in contexts where learners have limited opportunities for target language practice, chatbots can become an invaluable resource. During the COVID-19 pandemic, social distancing rules have meant that availability of online conversation practice has gained further prominence. Second, chatbots are patient conversational partners who do not lose patience when learners repeat the same content, make the same mistakes, or ask the same questions. Third, learners who experience second language anxiety find communicating with chatbots stress-free. Learners know that they can communicate freely without being judged by the chatbot and take as much time as they need to construct their expressions. Finally, chatbots can provide immediate correction or seek clarification when they do not understand learner input. Yin and Satar (2020) observed that chatbots, particularly if designed for pedagogical purposes, can engage in meaning-negotiation with the learners and elicit modified output especially around lexical items that cause misunderstanding (see Yin & Satar, 2020) for example, meaning-negotiation sequences). While most available bots afford written communication, there is evidence that written chat resembles speaking practice and can transfer to spoken conversation development (Satar & Özdener, 2008).

Potential issues

Unfortunately, conversational agents also have several limitations. Once the initial novelty wears out, chatbot responses can become predictable, redundant, or irrelevant, which can cause learners to lose interest. Second, learners may be annoyed if they repeatedly receive generic responses (e.g. I don't know),

Chapter 21. Speaking with machines

or answers which do not make sense. Third, chatbots have limited capacity to engage in affective communication and give useful feedback. Fourth, they do not present an ideal model for communication as they tend to lack human interactional features (e.g. fillers, false starts, and hesitations). Fifth, chatbots are designed for specific tasks, and are not flexible conversational partners. This poses a challenge for teachers in utilising chatbots for language learning. Teachers would need to identify a specific chatbot designed to support a certain task, for instance a customer services chatbot for a context in which a learner is required to purchase goods or services.

As chatbots improve, other issues also emerge. As more capable pedagogical bots are developed, language teachers may suffer increased anxiety around the fear of being replaced by machines. When chatbots begin to resemble humans too much, they create feelings of unease not only in teachers, but also in learners. Additionally, chatbots can pose dangers to online safety and cause ethical dilemmas. There are fake social media accounts linked to bots or fraudulent applications, which are called spam or scam bots. Advice on how to identify such fake accounts can be found online. When chatbots pretend to be human (rather than identifying themselves as intelligent agents), ethical concerns also arise. This was the case for Google's Duplex when it was introduced in May 2018.

Looking to the future

> Progress in AI and conversational agents is at an unprecedented speed regarding their appearance, functionality, linguistic accuracy, ability to offer specific responses, and to represent a personality. The chatbot Eugene Goostman is one example of a chatbot with a personality, which imitated a 13 year-old humorous Ukranian boy. A new development to look out for is Google's new AI: Meena. In January 2020, it was announced that compared to modern interactional bots, Meena will be "a Human-like Open-Domain Chatbot […] based on a 2.6 billion parameter end-to-end

> trained neural conversational model [potentially leading] to many interesting applications, such as further humanizing computer interactions, improving foreign language practice, and making relatable interactive movie and videogame characters" (Adiwardana et al., 2020) While we can expect to interact with chatbots more often in our daily lives in the coming years, it will be important to incorporate ethical discussions around chatbot interaction in language and teacher training classes as part of digital literacy skills frameworks. We need further research and practice reports investigating the interactional engagement of different groups of language learners with various types of interaction bots to capitalise on this freely available technology, and ensure future successful incorporation of bots in second language learning and teaching.

References

Adiwardana, D., Luong, M. T., So, D. R., Hall, J., Fiedel, N., Thoppilan, R., Zi, Y., Kulshreshtha, A., Nemade G., Lu, Y., & Le, Q. V. (2020). Towards a human-like open-domain chatbot. *arXiv preprint*. arXiv:2001.09977

Satar, H. M., & Özdener, N. (2008). The effects of synchronous CMC on speaking proficiency and anxiety: text vs. voice chat. *The Modern Language Journal, 92*(4), 595-613. https://doi.org/10.1111/j.1540-4781.2008.00789.x

Shultz, M., & Heift, T. (2013). Intelligent CALL. In M. Thomas, H. Reinders & M. Warchauer (Eds), *Contemporary computer-assisted language learning* (pp. 249-266). Bloomsbury.

Yin, Y., & Satar, M. (2020). English as a foreign language learner interaction with chatbots: negotiation for meaning. *International Online Journal of Education and Teaching (IOJET), 7*(2), 390-410. http://iojet.org/index.php/IOJET/article/view/707

Resources

Advice on how to identify fake accounts: https://www.technologyreview.com/2018/07/18/141414/how-to-tell-if-youre-talking-to-a-bot/

Chapter 21. Speaking with machines

Behind the mic: the science of talking with computers: https://www.youtube.com/watch?v=yxxRAHVtafI

Chatbots – a beginners guide: https://www.youtube.com/watch?v=JGIFN9HHl04

The case for Google's Duplex: https://www.technologyreview.com/2018/06/27/141823/google-demos-duplex-its-ai-that-sounds-exactly-like-a-very-weird-nice-human/

Watch two chatbots talk with each other: https://www.youtube.com/watch?v=WnzlbyTZsQY

Try out some chatbots yourself:

ELIZA: https://www.eclecticenergies.com/psyche/eliza

Mitsuku: https://www.pandorabots.com/mitsuku/

Alice: https://www.pandorabots.com/pandora/talk?botid=b8d616e35e36e881

If you are interested in creating your own bot you can try this: https://home.pandorabots.com/home.html

TeachMeets
continuing professional development for teachers by teachers

Jane Basnett[1]

Potential impact	high
Timescale	short term
Keywords	TeachMeet, Twitter, continuing professional development, Guerrilla CPD, unconference

What is it?

A TeachMeet (TM) is a form of free Continuing Professional Development (CPD) that originated in 2006 in Scotland, and has since been known under many guises; guerrilla CPD, unconference, and bottom-up CPD. The forefather of this form of CPD is educational consultant Ewan McIntosh, who originated these meetings for those educators in primary and secondary schools who wanted to share ideas and talk expressly about teaching. From the very first TM, which took place on the peripheries of an educational conference, there have been certain characteristics that define this teacher-led CPD. The by-line for a TM is 'teachers sharing ideas with teachers'. As this strapline suggests, the presenters at a TM are also the attendees; they are there to learn from each other at a utilitarian meeting. The presentations, often described as micro or nano presentations, are short, and there is 'break-out time' when attendees can get together, learn more from each other, and share and develop ideas. Indeed, as Bennett (2012) suggests "the value of a conference is not the keynotes or even the workshops, but the conversations that happen in the corridor or over coffee" (p. 24).

---

1. Downe House School, Thatcham, United Kingdom; basnettj@downehouse.net

How to cite: Basnett, J. (2021). TeachMeets: continuing professional development for teachers by teachers. In T. Beaven & F. Rosell-Aguilar (Eds), *Innovative language pedagogy report* (pp. 139-144). Research-publishing.net. https://doi.org/10.14705/rpnet.2021.50.1249

The same can be said for TMs, which is why, from its inception, there is always a moment for attendees to come together over food to discuss and make connections, which is also another important part of the TM movement.

Initially, TMs were accused of overly focusing on technological innovation, but, over time, TMs have evolved so that the majority of events now have a focus on a specific topic or theme, providing a more focused CPD experience.

Despite all these changes, the essence of a TM has remained largely the same. A TM very often has a facilitator, who will organise the timings and the theme of the meeting, if there is one. As Almond, Johnston, and Millwood (2018) point out in their study of the evolution of the TM phenomenon, one third of meetings follow

> ❝ 'the build it and they shall come' lead, and reflect an event which invites variety in presentation topics by those who volunteer to present" (p. 239).

From their genesis, TMs have largely been advertised on online backchannels (social media such as Twitter) both before an event to gain an audience – and, thus, presenters who will share ideas – and during the event itself. A TM will have a name that hooks in the participants (such as Learning Rocks from TM Clevedon https://www.smore.com/b082-teachmeet-clevedon) and a hashtag with which to promote the event during the proceedings. Such an approach makes for a very inclusive type of CPD for teachers all around the world.

Example

An example of a themed event on Modern Foreign Languages (MFL) is #dhlang15 TM, where educators from languages departments from all key stages of primary and secondary school came together to discuss language-focused ideas. The presenters tackled themes and ideas that could be adapted by all parties in their own circumstances (Figure 1).

Figure 1. Official Twitter poster for #dhLang15 MFL TM

The event was advertised locally and on social media, in particular *Twitter*, with the facilitator garnering financial support for the event via sponsorships that were largely language-specific. Among others, thisislanguage and VocabExpress, both companies that provide online resources for language teachers, were popular sponsors of the event. The participants and presenters were sought out and invited in the same way, via Twitter. On the night itself, participants used the hashtag to share pertinent ideas that were relevant to the language classroom.

Chapter 22. TeachMeets

Thus, the event reached well beyond the 70 participants in the room, with 'audience members' coming from all over the world.

Presentation topics ranged from technological tools that can enhance language learning to how to encourage more spontaneity in speaking. One presentation that had a particular influence on many in the audience was based on the importance of drilling and practising in modern languages. The ideas expounded upon in this two-minute nano presentation were forceful and to the point, and were a useful reminder for the audience of repetition in language learning.

Benefits

The variety of topics discussed at a TM allows attendees to learn about differing pedagogical approaches in use and to consider further teaching ideas that are being applied in the language classroom. For example, tricky skills, such as creative writing or fluency in speaking, are often considered, and provide some much-needed insight into how others tackle these areas. Participants can leave with real ideas and resources that they can use right away in their own classrooms. In addition, the chance to chat with colleagues at a TM gives a much-needed opportunity for educators to collaborate with and learn from like-minded individuals. Some even take the opportunity to let off steam about educational issues and policies, which might not be possible in traditional forms of CPD. Not to mention the lone voice scenario: if you are the only teacher of a subject, such as German, a TM provides an invaluable opportunity to discuss your subject with others. The general atmosphere at a TM enhances the whole experience, and attendees often come away feeling energised. Additionally, they are rife with opportunities to build community and personal learning networks with other educators from other institutions who are similarly motivated to enhance their teaching.

Potential issues

Given that the speakers are drawn from the attendees, it is never really possible to gauge the quality of the speaker beforehand. In themed evenings, some ideas may not be transferable to every context, and it would be fair to say that some attendees may gain more than others, for whom the TM presentations might propound ideas that are already commonplace in their classrooms or simply not relevant.

Looking to the future

> Even if attendees come away with just one idea to work with in their classrooms, the benefits of TMs outweigh any potential drawbacks. The recent pandemic has driven TMs online, and these have been very successful, with attendee numbers in the hundreds. In fact, the ability to connect with educators further afield is a positive side effect of this new approach; the greater field of educators willing to contribute and participate means that the quality of presentations is even greater, the proceedings are slicker, and attendees can more easily fit the TM into their busy schedules. This is to say nothing of the reduced costs for those who would normally have travelled to the TM and the refreshment costs placed on the organisers.
>
> The desire for informal discussion, which is a feature of TMs can be met via the online chat function of whatever forum is used for the event and on social media via the hashtag. Given the cynicism and general apathy that can surround traditional CPD, and that teachers increasingly want to take responsibility for their own learning, TMs are most definitely here to stay, and are likely to continue to getting stronger in this new online format.

References

Almond, M., Johnston, K., & Millwood, R. (2018). Self-organised professional development - the TeachMeet phenomenon. *Proceedings of INTED2018 conference, Valencia, Spain.* https://doi.org/10.21125/inted.2018.1036

Chapter 22. TeachMeets

Bennett, E. (2012). Teachmeets: guerrilla CPD. *Educational Developments, 3*(4), 23-27. http://eprints.hud.ac.uk/id/eprint/16312/

Resources

Anderson, M. (2013, January 12). What is a TeachMeet anymore? *ICT Evangelist*. https://ictevangelist.com/what-is-a-teachmeet-any-more/

EdPuzzle, a demo by Lauren Crawley at Downe House Teach Meet 2020 #EduDH20: https://vimeo.com/421256890/64ab51e8c8

#pracped16 TeachMeet: https://magsamond.com/2016/11/27/pracped16-practical-pedagogies-in-toulouse/

#dhlang15 TeachMeet : https://dhtm.wordpress.com/2015/06/21/dhlang15/

Author index

A
Absalom, Matt ix, 97

B
Basnett, Jane ix, 139
Beaven, Ana ix, 43
Beaven, Tita viii, 1
Buendgens-Kosten, Judith x, 103

C
Carreres, Ángeles x, 83

F
Fuertes Gutiérrez, Mara x, 29

G
Germain-Rutherford, Aline xi, 91
Gimeno-Sanz, Ana xi, 49
Godwin-Jones, Robert viii, xxii
Gutiérrez, Begoña F. xi, 17

H
Helm, Francesca xii, 11

M
MacKinnon, Teresa xii, 57
Martínez-Arboleda, Antonio xii, 77

N
Noriega-Sánchez, María xiii, 83

O
O'Dowd, Robert xiii, 17

P
Pegrum, Mark xiii, 115
Pérez Castillejo, Susana xiv, 121
Phipps, Alison xiv, 5
Plutino, Alessia xv, 35
Pujolà, Joan-Tomàs xv, 109

R
Rosell-Aguilar, Fernando viii, 1

S
Satar, Müge xv, 133
Shanks, David xvi, 69
Sumner, Josh xvi, 63

U
Underwood, Joshua xvi, 127

V
Vinagre, Margarita xvii, 23

www.ingramcontent.com/pod-product-compliance
Lightning Source LLC
Chambersburg PA
CBHW022012160426
43197CB00007B/392